11.95

Jack and Dorothy

By the same author:
A Square Peg (Mercier Press/Marino Books, Dublin) 1997
Late Developer (Seerendipity, Darlington) 2005

Jack and Dorothy
Letters from the Front 1915–17

Elizabeth McCullough

SERENDIPITY

First published in 2005 by
Serendipity
37/39 Victoria Road
Darlington

British Library Cataloguing-in-Publication data
A catalogue record for this book is available from the British Library
ISBN 1-84394-171-6
Printed and bound by The Cromwell Press

Foreword

May 2005

My mother was a very reticent woman: however over the years it has become apparent that the death of her fiancé left a deeper scar than she ever revealed in conversation. Ninety years after his death, I have decided to publish the letters he wrote to her and her mother, as well as relevant excerpts from the diary she kept in the year following his death. It is poignant that Jack's last letter, dated 11 December 1917, ends: "You're all the world to me, Dorothy."

Jack and his friend Haddon express deep commitment to peace, strongly held principles and, in Haddon's case, religious faith. All emerge with dignity, and I have not lightly undertaken this task.

North Berwick, Scotland

Dedication and Acknowledgements

In memory of my late mother, Dorothy, and her fiancé Jack. I should also like to include my father's half-brother, Lieut. Hugh Stevenson who was killed in action at Passchendaele Ridge on 10 October 1917, just ten weeks before Jack died of his wounds.

Hugh's cousins, Lieut. Ernest McClure and Lieut. Leonard William Hugh Stevenson, MC, had lost their lives on 1 July 1916: the latter's name is recorded on the Thiepval Memorial, Somme, France.

Publication of this volume has been aided by Brian Ross and Bob Jones, who helped with computer technology, and Images of Morningside, Edinburgh, who dealt carefully with irreplaceable family photographs.

On the Isle of Raasay, thanks are due to Val Corey, who showed interest and did proof reading; also Roger Hutchinson who encouraged me to persist in my efforts to find a publisher.

John. S. Buggs.

Prologue

The extreme youth of Jack and Dorothy in this doomed relationship is evident in many ways; as is his awareness of the fleeting nature of life, missed opportunities, and the folly of war. He, perforce, is maturing more rapidly than his *enfant* Dorothy. He is a committed Home Ruler, she an Ulster Unionist (although quite why is unclear, considering the family came to Ulster as late as 1910 from a background in Cumberland and Newcastle-upon-Tyne). The fact that Dorothy was sent, at the impressionable age of fourteen, to a private school in a staunchly Protestant part of Belfast may, despite her tendency to non-conformity, have something to do with it. It is surprising to learn that she was not commited to women's suffrage, but I suspect there was little discussion of politics or international affairs in the home, and the Empire concept was deeply ingrained in her family.

Although Jack mentions the Easter Rising of 1916, its causes and likely consequences, at some length, no hint is revealed of what Dorothy thought. Nor is any mention made of the Russian Revolution in 1917.

Self-effacing, insecure, and frustrated by his inability to express thoughts and emotions adequately, Jack continues to the end repeating "I am afraid", "I am sorry", "Somehow I can't write today", using facetious remarks to disguise his real feelings. Nearing the end of the letters there is a marked improvement when he reveals a distant, tortured, relationship with his mother. "As usual I got the blame." Widowed, with four children, she married a Mr Patton, of the Bank House, Waring Street, Belfast. Dorothy's diary, where she records visits to the Bank, names Jack's sisters Nina and Ledlie, but contains no reference to his mother. It is noteworthy that the letters of condolence from his regiment are addressed to his sister Nina.

He has trouble with the use of adverbs – preferring 'awful' where it is not appropriate, and difficulty when it comes to a choice between 'to' and 'too'! Both he and Dorothy always meticulously record the time. "I am writing this at 11 p.m.," and "Jack came at 3.15 and left about 10.30"! He does not seem to have absorbed the attitudes typical of the parochial culture from which he came, and one senses a restless soul who needs encouragement to stretch the bounds of conformity. Dorothy, although rebellious, was shackled by the moral constraints of her upbringing, and too insecure herself to be of much help. Although he scarcely figures in the letters, she was deeply attached to her father: a religious man, whose own father had been a Baptist, he had strict ideas on family values and the emancipation of women. Her mother, although she emerges quite well from the letters, was a martinet, who ran the home with military precision: Dorothy's diary mentions frequent onslaughts on

Dorothy (centre) with friends, March 1906

various rooms in the family abode with which, despite there being a maid, she was expected to assist. Further education, other than continued piano and dance studies and a course at the College of Art, were deemed sufficient preparation for marriage. It is surprising that she was permitted to work at Mackie's foundry, and that she seems not to have sensed the irony of making shell-cases, albeit to be directed at the enemy.

There is underlying sexual frustration in the references to having been "rough" and inconsiderate, and exhortations that Dorothy employ self-will to deter what Jack refers to as his "brutish nature". Dorothy's preference for just remaining "chums" indicates another aspect of the relationship, but her interest in all things mechanical and enthusiasm for motor vehicles was genuine, and persisted throughout her long life. Always elegant and dressed in the height of fashion, she designed and made her own clothes. A lot of her slender income was spent on dress materials and shoes.

Jack's preference for a "good yarn" reveals something of his literary inclinations, and I suspect Dorothy was trying to widen his interests. She was a devotee of Somerville & Ross, H. G. Wells, Kipling, 'Sapper' and the Sherlock Holmes stories, later in life graduating to Dorothy L. Sayers, Anthony Trollope, Mary Renault and Robert Graves. Jack's enthusiasm for Rugger – had their romance not been so brutally terminated – would have been divisive. Although Dorothy dutifully attended matches when Jack was on home leave, she notes the cold misery of the scene, and her martyrdom to chilblains.

The last section of the letters repeatedly reverts to Jack's wish to transfer to the R.F.C. His obsession was woefully misunderstood by Dorothy and her mother, whose views were insensitive to the real nature of the man. Dorothy is indeed an *enfant*, and she and her mother ill-informed about the risks of flying, as opposed to front-line warfare. I imagine that, with hindsight, Dorothy may well have suffered agonies of guilt about her attempts to dissuade him; and was probably haunted by the thought that the future he hoped for, 'to be a qualified pilot would always be something' (p. 93) might have been realised had he been encouraged to follow his inclinations.

In a way it is sad to read how soon she is "having a great time" with the American naval officers who were stationed at Culmore near Greencastle in the summer of 1918. Between then and October 1922, when she married my father, there were a number of admirers, most of whom shared her passion for motor cycles. The marriage was a disaster, owing to my father's alcoholism, which she did her best to conceal for many years. Ultimately a legal separation was agreed shortly before my untimely birth. Dorothy's attitude to men was irreparably damaged by this experience; she retained her interest in clothes, however, retaining a remarkably youthful appearance for many years, but never again risked emotional involvement with a man.

Notes

Drumaweir House, Greencastle, Inishowen, Co. Donegal, and the boathouse referred to in Dorothy's diaries remain virtually unchanged: the property is now owned by Brian Friel. Dorothy's friend was Gertrude Stevenson, daughter of the hotel's owners, referred to as Gertie and not to be confused with Jack's sister of the same name.

Richmond Lodge which Dorothy attended, as did Jack's three sisters Nina, Gertrude and Ledlie, was an outstandingly good school. The Headmistress was Miss Violet Nairn, a progressive woman, widely respected by parents and pupils alike. My mother sometimes referred to the achievements of past pupils, among them Helen Waddell, author of *Heloise and Abelard*, and Charlotte MacIldooey who 'escaped' the confines of Belfast for the theatrical world of London, marrying George Lansbury by whom she had a daughter, Angela, of TV reknown.

Drumaweir House, Greencastle

The End of the Story

Losses in the Ranks – Belfast News-Letter, 20 December, 1917

Second-Lieut. J. S. RIGGS, R.G.A., who died of wounds on the 19th inst., was the only son of the late Mr James L. Riggs and Mrs Robert Patton, Ulster Bank House, Waring Street, Belfast, and a grandson of the late Mr John Stephenson Riggs, of Sunnymount, Armagh. He joined the Royal Engineers at the outbreak of war, and trained as a despatch rider with the 15th Division in England, going overseas a year later. In June last he obtained a commission in the Royal Garrison Artillery, and went to France in August. He was dangerously wounded on the 18th inst., and died, as stated, on the following day. Before entering the army he was serving his time as an engineer in the firm of Workman, Clark, and Co., Limited. He was an old boy of the Royal Belfast Academical Institution.

This letter from France dated 2 January, 1918
is addressed to my grandmother

My Dear Mrs Kendall,

I am so glad you have written for it has, as it were, broken the ice. I've wanted to write to Miss Kendall, but I could not bring myself to it – in plain English I was frightened of the pain of the task. Your letter has taken that away, for I have the honour to join you in your sorrow, for I think we were more friendly than any other pair on the battery. I was drawn to him at the start away in Flanders where he came fresh to us, and since then we have been as much together as was possible.

Here, for instance we built a dugout for two, and it was chiefly due to his ingenuity that it was the envy of the other officers. When we moved a few miles north we were separated for he stopped with a section along with the senior subaltern. When I came back from leave on Dec. 4, I was quite joyful to hear I was to go there as the senior Sub. was going on leave. So I rejoined him, and found the place getting "unhealthy" as we call it owing to the Boche shelling it. We were busy building and digging other quarters for that very reason. His fearlessness was great. The Captain was there a day or two before I got there and seemed glad to get away. I lay awake several nights listening to the"Krump" of shells close by our billet and Jack's only reply if I spoke was to turn over and say "Oh they'll get us if they try long enough" while I determined to clear out into new dugouts as soon as possible. The morning Jack was wounded I was away. We took turns every four days, spending 24 hours at an observation post in a much-straffed part of the line, and it was my turn there. I had finished the time and been relieved, and walking "home" could see our billets being shelled. I never dreamt of anything serious for I knew there were good shelters handy, quite shell proof. As I approached, I saw things had been badly knocked about, but could hardly believe my ears when told that my friend had been hit. The men were quite nervous as you may understand for they had been bombarded about 4 hours continuously which is an ordeal even when one is in comparative safety. Jack had sent all the men to cover and was apparently at the telephone in the BC post when he was hit by two splinters. We all thought his "tin hat" had saved him for his head wound was fairly light and the other on his shoulder was not awfully serious. The men found him and carried him into shelter and as soon as the shelling permitted took him to the dressing station. There he was attended to and at once sent off to a clearing station. He was characteristically cheerful, smiling and saying to the men "Cheerio Boys I'm off to Blighty this time". All this had happened when I got back but I got hold of the Doctor, as I was anxious; and he also was cheerful not expecting anything tragic at all. After this, you may imagine the shock I had when a telephone message came through of the fatal termination. The major went round to the Clearing Station himself, and found that the wound had become gangreneous – supposedly through gas poisoning – and that he became unconscious and passed quietly away.

He was a great favourite with the men, and although we get wretchedly callous out here, you would have been surprised at the sadness caused generally, at the tragic news. Personally, although I'd been the unwilling spectator of many tragedies out here, I felt a kind of stubborn refusal to believe the news that I can't explain. I can join you in your admiration of him, and echo your words that he was "a straight, clean-souled lad" – a greater compliment than I think you realise. For, while I marvel at the bravery and cheerful bravery too, of the boys out here, one can't be blind and deaf to things that are very general, and that are far from being either straight or clean.

I sincerely hope I have not said too much. If I have, please put it down to my desire to tell you all I could – though letters are feeble instruments to that end. Anything I can answer I shall be so pleased to do. Perhaps one other thing I might add. He was very very tired of the war. He often used to jokingly make fun of my daily letter to my wife and kiddie, but he longed for the war to end and peace to come – it was his daily complaint. He hated the whole thing and wanted to get back home, even stronger than most of us.

I'm afraid I have not been able to give much comfort in my letter. I pray that Our Father may send that.

I am, Yours very sincerely, John L. Haddon 239(3) Battery

Dated 2 January, 1918 from John L. Haddon
to my mother

My Dear Miss Kendall,

Now the way is somewhat clearer, will you please allow me to offer my sincerest sympathy at this time? I recall with mixed feelings, the conversation we had when he asked me to share some of the dainties you sent him. I pointed out those little feminine touches, jokingly, which I recognised – for I knew what was behind the neatly packaged box. He used to laugh at my fatherly way of talking to him, but I felt so much older than him somehow, and he didn't mind really.

I know too well from my own experience, the apparent coldness of words in times like these – but, believe me, I share your pain. May Our Heavenly Father give you the comfort that no one else can, is the prayer of Jack's comrade.

J. L. Haddon

P.S. I would have answered before but I have been away for a week.

10 February, 1918

My Dear Miss Kendall,

This is the first opportunity I have had of answering your letter. We have had a poor time the last month – 2 officers in Blighty per hospital train and 2 per leave train. At one period of about a week there were actually only 2 of us to run the show.

May I answer your last question first? As far as I know no one saw him after admission to the Central Clearing Station. It was a long way from here and when the major went over in the car it was too late.

As to the pictures – exactly as surmised – note the men picking their way through the lovely mud. In two of them the bike is Jack's and the officers are Captain Newberry and a Mr Cauntrip belonging to another lot. One is interesting showing Jack's bed in the distance and mine in the corner. The stove he made is on the right. You understand why I cannot say anything at all of a "full" nature? If I get a chance when I am home on leave (or for good) I'll give a fuller description.

Yours very sincerely, J. L. Haddon

25 January, 1918

Dear Miss Kendall,

I was pleased to get your letter, chiefly because you assure me that I didn't say too much. As to the copies [*photographs*] I shall be only too pleased to name all I know. Returning them will be the difficulty, and will have to be done as before. However, that will not be insurmountable.

I have not heard of any reaching him before and I'm sure he would have shown me them if they had come. There are certain necessary formalities to go through with regard to his kit, but it is all inventoried and sealed up and will reach his people all right in due course. We are not allowed to send anything private – which on the whole is perhaps a good thing.

We have had a few days "rest" lately, and I missed JS very much, for though others are jolly and all that, they don't seem to "fit" like he did. We had 9 days, but the middle 3, I had to return with some men and we had a rather poor time – it is a miracle really that one team at least were not quite put out. Now we have returned and have already sent some off to Blighty. It really gets on one's nerves however one may smile and joke about it. I was only thinking today, as I patched up one of our boys, what possibilities there are of pain and suffering. And I am so pleased that _that_ at least was spared him.

Only a night or two before he and I were wordily disputing about whether the Church as such was worth keeping going. I could talk easily to him on such subjects although we rarely agreed as far as the surface of things go; and he liked it too. I often used to unload on him scraps of my pet religious theories – by no means awfully heterodox. There are not many men one can do that with. They either slide off into other topics or "have no use" for such things.

His great forte was tinkering with the motor bikes. He simply was a magician as far as they were concerned, doctoring them wonderfully. He was the most expert "rough-rider" of a motor bike I knew – riding over any sort of ground in any sort of weather and always getting there. In the same way he used to manage to make things so comfortable. He made a fine stove in our dugout and used to delight in getting it jolly hot too. Then he got an acetylene bike lamp, and put it up as a light in the dugout – so that it was quite the "show" habitation in the battery. He really delighted in doing things and inactivity bored him fearfully. I suppose you knew that he was leaving us in order to become an airman? He had quite set his mind on it though I gave him no encouragement or otherwise as far as that is concerned. I am so sorry about it all. As you say words seem so futile that they almost make one angry at their feebleness.

Yours very sincerely, J. L. Haddon

The following letter written by Haddon on Jack's behalf dated 22 October, 1917 helps to explain the nature of the friendship:

Dear Miss Dorothy,

John S. is "fed up" tonight – a not unusual state in the Army I'm afraid. He has it so bad in fact that to stir him up a bit I have actually threatened to write his letter for him. I'm afraid it is one of those easily made offers that one regrets at leisure – in fact I'm already in difficulties as perhaps you can see. In fact as I begin to realise my impudence I also begin to blush – which perhaps doesn't matter so much as you are so far away that my blushes are invisible. Well, I had better begin in the official style of the field postcard only translating it into 3rd person singular (I think that is what it is called). "He is quite well", "He has <u>not</u> been admitted to hospital" (N.B. they wouldn't have him), "He has received a letter from you dated . . .", "Letter follows at first opportunity". At present he is suffering hardship as a good soldier by sitting in slippered ease in front of a blazing fire. Still he deserves it for last night he was shivering in an Observation Post in the trenches wrapped in a topcoat – one consequence of whch was that he slept all day while I have been hard at work. Asking your forgiveness,

I am, Yours sincerely, J. L. Haddon

20 Casualty Clearing Station, B.E.F
20 December, 1917

Dear Miss Riggs,

Your brother – 2nd Lieut. J. S. Riggs – 239 Siege Batt – R.G.A. – was admitted here on the 18th late, and died last night at 10.40 p.m. He had a very badly fractured skull and severe wounds of the shoulder, and a fractured humerus too.

He was in a very critical condition on admission – but conscious, only poor boy he was too ill to leave any messages. He rapidly lost consciousness and at the time of his death was unconscious. He will be buried today by one of our Chaplains who will write to you. His personal belongings will be sent off from here to the War Office and will be forwarded by them.

It must be a dreadful blow to you, but I hope a little comfort to know that he died in a British Hospital, where all that could possibly be done for him was. With deepest sympathy from the Staff.

Yours faithfully,
Eva Schofield, Sister in Charge

20 December, 1917

Dear Miss Riggs,

It is with the greatest sorrow that I have to inform you of the death of your brother, which occurred yesterday – from wounds received the day before. He was in his billet when a shell pitched outside, and splinters hit him in the head and shoulder. He was taken straight to hospital but died the next night. I tried to get to the funeral, but arrived too late. The chaplain who buried him is writing to you.

I cannot say how deeply we deplore his loss. He was a great favourite with everyone. He is buried in a military cemetery on The Arras-Bucquoy road.

Will you please accept the sympathy of the whole of the battery. I cannot say more – words seem so futile. If there is anything else I can do, please ask.

Sincerely yours,
E. Allen, Major R.G.A., Comdg 239 Siege Battery

The Beginning 1915

The Distillery – France
28 July, 1915

Dear Miss Kendall,

I hope you don't mind me calling you 'Miss' – I really think you deserve it for addressing me as 'Jack' in your first letter – I hope it won't be your last! You are welcome to the buttons – they were not essential to my apparel! I don't know any little French girls, but a kind friend (a fellow motor-cyclist) translated it for me – he says it means "the jolly old rig-out" – idiomatic rendering of "*tout ensemble*" what? But then he is very clever. I was delighted to hear that you had some manners – I always suspected it, in spite of what people told me. Thank goodness we are not worried by Flag Days here, although we encountered one in Southampton on our way out: I bought several, being quite unable to resist the charms of the pretty English ladies.

I should love to have a pair of mittens, especially if you had knitted them. I am sure they aren't awful. While the weather is still warm, I could use them as bed-socks, or respirators, and when winter arrives they will be fine for riding the bike. Your suggestions are excellent, but they have their drawbacks – I don't smoke a pipe, and I don't snore, so, if you don't object, I shall adopt my own methods. Since you ask my opinion of our grub, I shan't give it you – you would probably be shocked, as I can't refrain from strong language when talking about it. Our chief amusement at present is watching aeroplanes – there is an aerodrome just near here, so we see a good many of them. Most evenings we can see them being shelled, but they generally get a comfortable distance from the explosions.

Another pastime is entitled "Baiting the Sergeant" – not our own particular one, but a fat, officious and altogether objectionable sergeant! He is really quite outside the outer edge, and we treat him accordingly – which he does not like. Therefore, with much amusement! He has one virtue, however, he does not quail before army grub; any amount of it vanishes down him in incredibly quick time. We are living a life full of danger – in fact, it is nothing short of marvellous that I have survived so far. Shells burst all round us (and particularly round me!) whenever we go out: bullets whistle by, and bombs explode in impotent fury on every side. And yet not a man has been hit. I am absolutely convinced that I owe my own safety to the fact that I always carry your letter about with me – it acts as a mascot of great power! So do write again soon, and then I shall be thoroughly protected from injury with two mascots! Besides, letters are very welcome out here – So –

Sincerely yours (your own phrase!)
John S. Riggs

9 October, 1915

Dear Dorothy,

I have now returned to the company. You'll be sorry to hear that Weaver has gone to hospital with skin trouble. I was over to see him yesterday but he didn't mention you. Strange. We were all to have been granted leave in turn, one a week, but late last night it was all cancelled as the Germans were attacking again. We are about 10 miles back supposed to be resting, but of course we might have to go up any time. I have been working very hard this morning getting a tarpaulin rigged up to shelter our machines – real hard work for a change. I wish we could get our food cooked so easily. We have a struggle with a Primus stove before we can get anything. We find it's quicker and better to cook ourselves than depend on the Army cooks. We have lost our sergeant now as he has gone back to base with skin trouble. Our worthy friend Don is acting sergeant and I expect he will get the job for good. I expect we'll be much better off now as he's not frightened of work – the last one was.

I understand that Nina is going to take your photo for me. Now this is really nice of her, and I hope you'll do her credit. Please remember that there are

Dorothy, her mother and sister Rosemary in the garden of Drumaweir House

two others who are most anxious to see you. Unfortunately their affections are already engaged so you needn't be expecting to find your photo next their hearts. Don has about a dozen already, still he doesn't object to as many more. His only trouble is the French language. He does not get on at all well with the French girls. It's time I started to tidy up our attic now. Everybody else has, but I've escaped so far. We have heaps of rats here and sometimes get quite a lot of excitement from them at night.

Sometimes when driven to it we post our letters at the post office where there is an uncensored bag for headquarters. Thus we have them censored by one of their staff officers instead of our own and it doesn't matter when the censor doesn't know you. I thought I was on duty now but have just discovered I'm not till eleven. A relief as I'll be able to get a wash and clean up now. You wouldn't believe how used we are to being dirty. We haven't any excuse just now but after going for days without washing or sleeping we got used to it. If we ever get back it will be a change to be clean, really clean. I know I'll be quite thin at first. On this job we've become so lazy that we go to sleep at any odd moment when we've nothing else to do, we roll in a blanket and go to sleep. It's a good plan as it's always uncertain how long you may get next time. Don has just finished his struggle with the stove to get some shaving water – I intend to bag some of it so you'll have to excuse me.

John S. Riggs

20 October, 1915

Dear Dorothy,

Indeed! Sir! So that is the result of not being un-offended. If so, when is it likely to be over? And I wish you would understand that one letter in two parts cannot be an answer to two letters. Several people I know seem to think this but it's wrong. You should know that there's nearly as much pleasure in getting a letter as there is in reading it. I'm sorry that I didn't always send the answers. I still think you asked for it. And my feelings weren't hurt. I know quite well I can't write a decent letter and you only wanted a letter from here. Still I am sorry if you are honestly offended (which I doubted at first) cos I admit we had no business to. I'm sorry to hear both from Nina and yourself that you seem to bully my eldest sister. You know she isn't as big as you and you shouldn't. Hit someone your own size next time. And what objection have you to me or any of us being a bit mad. Being serious wouldn't do us any good at all at all. So we choose to play the fool instead. Y.O. means our headquarters. Being 15th letter of alphabet headquarters are nearly always referred to as Y.O. And the second letter begins my dear Sir. Does this indicate any relenting or change of attitude. Also it is an honor for me to write. I am conceited enough to think so in any case "girls aint no use". I wouldn't depend if I were you on my getting leave for you to say things. It would only be six days and most of that would be travelling and if I were deaded I wouldn't hear which would be a pity. You tell us all about it and if I'm offended you'll hear all about it too! The best way for the photo would be to use a film of 8 on a bright day using the 1/25 shutter speed and the largest or second largest stop (f5.6 or 8) you can believe me we are most anxious to see photo even if it was thrust on me. So get on with it. I'm afraid there's a bitterness and unkindness under your letter that I don't like, I've had a letter from the Dean and I'll put him onto you to reform you when I'm answering. So you know if he calls. And there isn't any need to stop. Use pencil when your ink gives out. [*All these letters have been scrawled in pencil on thin paper, sometimes it would seem on an uneven surface.*]

John S. Riggs

19 November, 1915

Dear Dorothy,

I'm sorry your last letter from me ended so suddenly but I had to go to bed in the dark that night. I won't add the usual phrase you seem so fond of using. The dress seems to be a success, you're sure you aren't being extravagant after all the warnings the Government has given. I thought meself they might make a start on themselves first. We have also an Archibald [*name of Dorothy's dog*] staying near us. Only his position is more useful than your chap. Chris spends his time in strafing German planes whenever they appear. He's really useful. Why did you place his portrait on the next page? You see I might have objected to his kissing Nina unless I'd looked hurriedly. I could complain about your writing considering my own. I'm writing at present on my knee and I've very wet feet. But I am astonished that you should have been so regular like. Surely

Jack with Rosemary, 1915

you have better . . . Weaver-Adams and meself having been passed out after a week or two on riding lessons were put on despatch riding on the brutes. We were getting on beautifully and then on the second or third day I decided to "go sick" with boils. Weaver was as bad so we went together. Most interesting time. First day told to wash, or in other words bathe our necks in hot water several times a day. Everyone in company convinced we were "lead swinging" (I don't know if you understand – means slacking). Third day we did get a doctor who had had some. Poulticed us and gave us lint and said continue the processes. Today we had first doctor again who said persevere so now we are nearly well again. Our friend Don has just remarked to Weaver Adams "How would you like to kiss Mademoiselle?" I think she understood so now he has some explaining to do. She understands quite a lot of English so you have to be careful. We'll be very grateful for anything you send. I think if you consult Nina she'll be able to tell you what not to but everything from home is very very welcome now. It's quite different from England when I used to get too much stuff altogether; I explained so they stopped sending. And now we are coming back slowly to the old state with a difference that we want it now. I'll stop now as I have several more to write.

John S. Riggs

24 November, 1915

Dear Dorothy

I'm sorry that this letter should be the last this evening as it will be short. I don't expect you to believe this after your remark about your letters not being welcome. They are what I said they were and if you don't believe it you needn't. In future I'll know you don't believe anything I say so I needn't be truthful any more. As it happens your cutting doesn't apply as you didn't star it or anything in your letters, I presume you didn't mean it. Anyway I'm rather mad as I hate being accused of lying when I'm not. If I had been I shouldn't mind. Only I feel I lower myself by being doubted when you haven't any right to doubt it. I'm afraid I can't even answer your questions this time let alone tell you anything interesting. Now if you had stuck to Weaver you would have been told heaps of things. Not truthful of course, but you don't expect that. This must be finished to go with the others so I must stop. I think anyway you have had an extra one anyway only you annoyed me this time (about nothing of course), and I couldn't resist telling you so. I'm afraid you <u>are</u> conceited.

J. Riggs

1 December, 1915

Dear Dorothy,

I don't think your mother understands the situation when she says you needn't write because you wrote a week ago. Irony! And when you admit you knew there was one from me waiting you. Of course I minded the shortbread. You'll be pleased to know it vanished in a flash. We mistook it for butter first and were surprised. But we can always raise butter some way. So we are deeply grateful. Honestly Dorothy – and <u>knots per hour</u> – you may not know this is incorrect. A speed of so many knots means so many feet <u>per hour</u>. So there isn't an extra per hour required. And why should it be swank on my part? I hope to be finished with nickel bits and stirrups but I'll put those up here somewhere. Well now you know what S is for [*middle name Stephenson*] perhaps you will address me by my first name again. I'm sorry to tell you and I know you'll be too that Weaver-Adams has left us. He's been hunting a commission for some time and it arrived the other day. So off he went. Ron encloses a little note and hopes you won't be offended.

We are very pleased with the small tokens you sent us. We filled a four gallon petrol tin with water to float the little duck and perched the chicken on the side. The rattle Professor Panting (who cuts hair in his spare time) performs on. Really your little parcel <u>was</u> most welcome – please believe this. I don't like writing it again and again but you might believe it. I haven't any motive in telling you lies. I was fearfully pleased to have a fellow Ulsterman from Banbridge come up in Weaver-Adams' place. We have now 6 Irish in a section of a dozen. And all Home Rulers. We have only 6 of the men who were at Borden? We can't be convinced that the new men are up to the standard of our old friends. The chief cause has been sickness. We are steadily losing through this. I don't suppose it will be long before we get one or two more.

Cpl Beckett is at present giving us a short review of all the latest music hall songs etc. I'm afraid the remarks are more forceful than polite. I have several more letters to write so you'll have to do with this for the present. I'm glad you saw that you couldn't send a parcel without a letter. I knew there would be a letter and went to bed quite certain I'd find it in the morning. I often carry a letter here for a bit so as to enjoy it in anticipation. They go much further that way.

John S. Riggs

P.S. Thanks for stopping the (perhaps) at the end of your letter – I don't ever say anything at the end. So don't think I'm being rude I think it best just to stop. J. B.

7 December, 1915

Dear Dorothy,

I'm sorry about your feelings, I didn't want that you know, but maybe as you've said it, it may be good for you. And like most girls of course you would make out that you're the injured person. You seem to think that all you have to do is "feed the heart" and all will be well. Well if I was English perhaps, but I'm not and if you insult me too deeply you know I'd feel compelled not to have any. I didn't say I wrote with my feet did I? What I meant was that I had wet feet, and I'll bet you don't write long letters with soaking feet. Next time you're writing (not me, someone else) just place your feet in a cold bath with shoes and stockings on and see how much you write.

Your silhouettes were very welcome and I thank you. Don was much interested and said they were very nice – and he's an expert. Why can't we have a proper photograph? I don't suppose you spent a happy birthday with toothache, so I won't wish you many happy returns. I, worse luck am 20 and I wish – no we won't talk of that. But 19 is an awful age isn't it, you must feel old. Honestly – good luck. Do you take a pride in finishing all your letters differently? You know you use such <u>big</u> words and I can't.

I believe we are to move on the 1st – this will mean an unsettled Xmas as we'll have to find a new billet etc. But we hear fables about 25% going on leave at once so we look forward to the move. But we daren't hope for leave too much or we'd be getting sick. You'll be sorry to hear that the DRs we are getting who come through the training depot aren't much good. They haven't any heart and are very frightened of work and getting lost. In Signal terms they're wash outs. Thank heavens I joined in time to escape the training centre and the base here. We at least had a tremendous time in England as we were with this division since August 1914 and its much better than just being sent up afterwards. Sorry I can't write any more just now. I have Mrs Menary to write to – she's just sent me a parcel.

J. S. Riggs

17 December, 1915

Dear Dorothy,

Received your last letter when we were busy on the move. Many thanks. We had to go over the day before with our machines and hut[?], return for motor [*illegible*] and take over horses the next day. When I arrived I had to get a gas engine and lighting plant running for that night. The last two days we've spent taking her down and adjusting. Tomorrow, with luck and the help of the Gods we'll have her running again.

I'm sorry you don't like being corrected. I admit it's nasty and I "only do it to annoy". Know where that comes from?

Yes, I'm afraid we are all Home Rulers here. There are some English Unionists though if that's any help. And I was told that Ireland had dropped politics for the war! Anyway please don't stop writing. You (as a Unionist) must show a better spirit than a mere Nationalist.

I'm a very poor letter writer and I wouldn't write at all if I didn't want to. You can, and do, write fine letters and I can't.

I'm sorry you seem so annoyed with me in your last letter. What's the trouble? Am I writing too often or your mother doesn't like it or what – please tell me.

Our sergeant went on leave some days ago and Don goes on the 22nd. I don't know when my turn comes but I suppose I'll be on this engine job and won't get it just yet. I won't tell the truth this time. Yes I will – I'm only writing to Nina after this. I feel really very crushed. Did you mean to or was it an accident? And I'm quite enough crushed now.

John Stephenson Riggs

1916

---

12 January, 1916

Dear Dorothy,

Glad you liked the cards. All I could get here and I had to get someone else to do that for me as I never got time to clean off the grease and go shopping. My word, shopping!

You must know I can't send things in return. To start with I can't and even if I could I don't suppose there is anything you couldn't get better at home. Many thanks for the foodstuff, but please don't say it's your duty: there's no duty in it. If you don't want to don't let duty move you.

Our Xmas went as well as could be expected. Rather spoilt by men having to leave hurriedly in the middle with despatches. I believe only about half the company were drunk. We didn't have turkey – several arrived about a week later, but their condition left much to be desired.

Yes, I'm afraid Nina wouldn't know the songs that Tommy likes. Most wild effect sometimes when you get about 30 or so all howling a song each giving his own idea of how it should go.

Interval while I was called to take the Captain out. You see we've built a sidecar after a style and it falls to me amongst other duties to drive it when needed. Some sidecar I assure you. It's a cause of trouble when I'm out with it empty as the French girls aren't troubled with shyness. The gas engine, thank you, is running. You just can't say much in its favour – a pump which it drives among other things fell to bits last night. As we are leaving here in a few days I'll just try to make it "carry on" – the next people can build it up again.

Sorry you have such an awful opinion of Home Rulers. I must say though that you meet more Irish Homerulers than Unionists out here. Anyway it's a humorous subject and keeps one alive to have argument now and again. God save Ireland.

As I said before we go back into action in a few days so Heaven knows when any leave will come. Still we are having quite a decent and exciting time on the whole just now, so I'm bearing up. It may interest you to know that I'm next in the section due to go, but as usual I'll be "too useful" and someone else will go instead. I don't really mind much because there's awfully little to go home for. If I could raise a light car now or a sidecar and machine there would be something in it. But such things can't be got for their weight in gold in Belfast during the war.

Must do some washing now. Oh yes I can do washing only its breeches this time, caps etc. and its petrol I use instead of water. Saves a lot of trouble

– 15 –

and dries much quicker. It's a bit expensive but I feed the engine on it after I've finished.

John S. Riggs

23 January, 1916

Dear Dorothy,

Many thanks for your last letter – it's the first I've had for ages now, and was of course doubly welcome. We are now in action once more and have the usual trouble in the way of shells etc. It would all be very funny indeed if it wasn't so deadly serious at the time to see the way everyone jumps for some cover when we hear one coming.

My job at present is the sidecar – it is used for officers, cable, linesmen and any old job they think of. In my spare moments I'm to assist the artificer. Sometimes I do nothing all day and other times I'm out all day and night. This type of job suits me fine because there's more variety in it.

As a matter of fact its 3/- a day we get – so there isn't a lot of cash around. Unless a shell lands on top of you (and then you won't be worried) you're all right. Anyway it provides something to talk about.

I object to the word duty chiefly because if I was told anything was my duty I didn't want to do it and wouldn't if possible.

I mentioned leave to the Skipper the other day. But I told him I wasn't in a hurry and would rather go when there wasn't anything doing – I reckon that means in a couple of months. And if you're going to be dignified when I get home that's another reason for not going. Really when I think of my last two leaves they were dull times. Everyone at home was bored to death by me and so was I, and yet they didn't like me going away. Well there wasn't anything to do at home or anywhere for that matter. Everyone I know is away and the politics it seems are dead – they at least were something to think about. Honestly I'm surprised that you object to the principles of Home Rule. If it had been the other way about that you objected to the class that wanted it, I could have understood. But the principles are above reproach. Honestly (again) I don't talk much about what I really believe in, but if one believes in any justice or freedom at all . . . Oh well, you be a Unionist, but this war showed how much the U.V.F. intended to fight. I have the most of my friends in the Ulster division and am told that just about half are the older ones who joined for Civil war against unarmed peasants. And when I said Home Rule I meant not Irish but people (England, Scotland, Wales) who passed opinions on it. It's not much good talking to a Unionist though. It surprised me to hear you were one as no real Unionist has a sense of humour or they would not have behaved as they did. God save Ireland.

Please I was in charge of that engine, not you, and it ran. Which is what I was there for. Also it had a rose head jet which required a fearful amount of stopping – also the engine ran on almost raw spirit.

I'm sorry to say I'd already written to my family when your letter came, and I mentioned that I didn't see much to go home for – sorry if you think I shouldn't have. It wasn't intended to hurt anyone's feelings least of all yours. It's not really essential for me to get a motor at home at all at all. And I can't see meself driving any girl anywhere just to get a motor. My lord! I'd pinch one somewhere off the street first. And me lady friends I'm afraid are few – my sisters and you.

Also I'm not a hero. Still you'll know that. I wasn't in the half that got drunk, but I expect that by next Xmas out here I will be. No Dorothy, you haven't said anything I want you to apologise for – I don't suppose you would anyway. And one thing I am sorry for, that's depressing you. It's not your fault and you've helped to cheer me up so often that I feel low down for hurting you if . . . oh, all right. No, you don't understand I'm afraid. I want something that requires some brain and strength to do – not just loafing about. You wouldn't really know me at all if I met you in the street. This whole letter seems depressing. Is it? Well there's so much to do and you won't be allowed to do it. This is a short life at the best and when petty little codes etc. are allowed to interfere it makes me mad. I won't write any more like that this time, but someone's got to have it and you often seem to be the only one I can write it to. So you are helping that way if its any consolation to you. You know you've been most fearfully decent to me in writing so often, and it annoys me to think that you might be doing it from some mistaken sense of duty. You're the only one again who writes any way often and which I can answer, but I'm afraid I can't be convinced its not from politeness. I wish this was more entertaining. I expect you'll be humorous on this remark next time. I'm aware I am a fool – I wasn't built for drawing rooms and I'm not happy there, so don't expect me to write too fanciful letters cos I can't. Wish I could get Weaver to write – he could tell this real well.

I've heard some of the best bits of news for a long time. At our Corps headquarters some miles back they are trying to get a Rugger team to play the French Flying men. Well, you may know or may not that I was Rugger mad and still am only now I'm out of training. Anyway they are to wire me when it's coming off. This war you know annoyed me because it stopped Rugger (well the Unionists had done that, or tried to but they didn't stop me). I had hopes by about this time of a cap for Ireland and was quite content with that very high ambitiion! Well, I'm sorry to say that's finished, these Huns you know – terrible people. Treat us like the wild Irish if they ever invaded us. As a matter of fact the average Tommy has a very good respect for the German Tommy, and they are getting on with the war which is something. I missed the parade tonight in order to write this uninterrupted. Fortunately one of the OR's reported all present so I've escaped. Pity.

John S. Riggs

11 February, 1916

Dear Dorothy,

Yours received two days ago. I'm sorry if you were worried about the shells. You must not. Anyway we have moved back now a bit as the Staff didn't like it. None of us of course liked it, but we are fairly well used to it by this time and it provides a pleasant sense of excitement when you always keep an ear cocked for one coming. I don't think I was exaggerating because I thought you knew we were just behind. Some of the places on the runs you can be sniped from. I have been up wind working parties when you do have to watch yourself. If it wasn't for little jaunts like these life would be very dull. It gets dull enough anyway sometimes. Anyway you needn't worry. You want to be very unlucky to try stopping shells. And I've come as close as I ever will and am still living. The next time will finish me.

No, I'm afraid the family circle doesn't appeal to me. It is dull here but it's awful there. I certainly understand you better about Home Rule. The politicians I admit on <u>both</u> sides are a bad lot. So that reduces it to a matter of principles again. I don't suppose we would get half either side claim. Besides I must admit that to me anyway its largely sentiment. Ireland was once a nation before the English rained trouble, and I would like to see her a nation again. I expect this sounds awful rot to a Unionist who hasn't any country except "The British Empire" – truly a fine thing to claim as a country!

I'm not likely to be offended on politics – much too amusing. I would give my real reasons for argument purposes. Anyway God Save Ireland.

The family did make an effort to entertain me last leave – they had a picnic. Mother knew I objected ever since meself and a friend had been sent home in disgrace (for nothing mind you, but that's another tale) from one of hers years ago. I said then I would never go to another. Well this time I discovered at the last moment it was to be an event to which I was to carry a ton of coals and sticks for a fire no less. Well I objected and didn't turn up. That was the first and last attempt and took place towards the end of my leave.

Aren't you aware that you are supposed to grow a face fungus in the army? And why (most important) do you object to it? You seem very sure – you needn't be polite to me – now why?

And don't unless you <u>want</u> me to have an attack of nerves refer to a <u>hard</u> day's work in the <u>Army</u>. It doesn't exist. You may be tired, but it's certainly not work.

I'm afraid I always have written just as I pleased. Many thanks for the permission just the same. I thought several times that Weaver might amuse you more. Weaver isn't quite in any world you know. He's done his bit in the ranks and knows the vast majority of officers have not and are thought little of by the men. Don't believe all the yarns you hear about the <u>love</u> the men have for their officers. There are some who wouldn't appear near the trenches in case their men might have an accident with their rifle!

I suppose you have heard that I am trying for the Flying Corps? I wouldn't say anything about it until sure – only you might be annoyed if I didn't tell you.

I still believe I'm down for leave soon but it might not be for a month or so. Maybe all leave will be stopped by then. The family of course are acting as if I was on the way.

John S. Riggs

24 February, 1916

Dear Dorothy,

I've been expecting to get leave any day, but every time it's been non est. We hear tonight that boats are stopped so it's unknown when the next leave date is. I've been the next for some time but they have always found someone else at the last moment and me another job. I'm glad you didn't stop writing just because there was a chance of leave. It's one of my great troubles in this war that I can't get anything except papers and magazines to read. I used to be a great reader of the madest yarns. I've read most of the <u>usual</u> books but the ones I liked best I'm afraid you would think mad.

You little know the motor-cyclists if you think that an order to grow fungus would make us do it. I haven't just because Skipper gave an order. The R.F.C. is off just at present as there is a long waiting list. Also you have to have a commission already if you can't fly. So I'm down for Irish Infantry as the infantry are the only other people who really meet the enemy.

I have been doing nothing at all the last week as I expected to be told any time to get on leave and of course I wouldn't work then. Some of the gentlemen of the section are seated round the fire with a tin whistle and a mouth organ playing hymes [sic]. Really fine when we never hear any music at all at all. Sorry, I'm "finished".

John S. Riggs

10 February, 1916

Dear Dorothy,

Yes, your remarks re magazines are very true. We find great amusement though in some of the yarns. You would only laugh and though they are impossible the theories mean a lot to me. So you wouldn't be satisfied on that point.

I haven't finished with the R.F.C. I hope. You have to finish an Infantry Officers' course first unless you can fly and I can't of course. It's only because I'm so fed up here. Yes, I was referring to meself, I do think well of myself I've such a lot of cause to.

You must know the chief reason I can't write home is that it means I'm really writing to everyone. And of course I can't tell anyone anything particular when everyone is knowing it: that's why I could write you because you were alone and not about a dozen. Then when Nina was called in that finished it. Not that I object at all. Only it's not the same. Also I didn't pretend you were showing letters around did I? I don't know what I've written a day later. I'm sorry for you being insulted so easily. <u>You</u> don't seem to know when I'm mad or not. I don't remember being with you yet. So you've that in store. I think I said I wouldn't apologize to you anymore because the first time you only wanted it for fun. So you can make that do. What does "obnoxious" mean?

Leave has been stopped I believe everywhere. And I don't want it when there is a chance of anything doing. And I'm not one to agitate for anything.

Also I mightn't be at home such a lot when I do get it.

You know I believe you are tired of writing. Why do you want to be reassured about once a week that I like your letters. I don't expect you to keep repeating things, so if you <u>don't</u> want to write for Heaven's sake don't and don't bother me about it. I do want to get your letters but don't write unless you want to. You really ask to be insulted you know. And I don't like threats. They only make me want to do things to see if the threats will be carried out. I have to stop now as I have a run to do.

John S, Riggs

The interval before the next letter is explained in Dorothy's 1918 diary:

Sunday 17 February: Quite a fine day but didn't go out being Sunday. Dusted drawing room – did some pen painting on candle shades. After dinner read. After tea music and reading. Exactly a year today since Jack came home. He came with Nina just after tea on Saturday. I'd been in bed with a cold and had just got up – they left early after asking me to go down there on Sunday.

Monday 18: Helped in the nursery [*sister Rosemary was 13 years her junior*]. Washed two blouses, sewed a bit at my voile blouse – got changed after dinner. Read and sewed till tea time. Just a year ago today I spent the afternoon and evening at the Bank. Jack came home with me and stayed to supper.

Tuesday 19: Helped with drawing room. Did a bit of sewing. Went down town to see why no butter had come – changed books and had a good chat with Miss Ferguson.

Wednesday 20: Mary told us just after breakfast she was ill and had to go to hospital – poor devil. I spent the morning rushing around after charwomen and going to registry office. Reading and sewing and housework in the evening. A year ago Jack came about 4.30 and we talked with a few pauses for breath till supper time when, after some pressure he stayed for supper. We arranged to go to the Tank film on Friday.

14 March, 1916

Dear Dorothy,

You see I'm writing in ink now. Really makes it much easier as my pencil was always lost or broken and if you borrowed one you might bet it would be too. I got this pen in a town some miles back from a mademoiselle who kept assuring me that everything was *très bon* and then giggled. Silly animals girls don't you think?

Many thanks for the shamrock. It was put in a tin box with a lump of mud to keep it fresh. Some more came this morning from family. Honour to be an

Irishman! This won't be long – really just thanking you for the shamrock. Are you still annoyed or cross. Don't worry you know or you'll grow old and maybe sensible! Which would be awful.

Great weather *aujourdhui*. Just the sort of day at home that I used to knock off work early and get the old buss out if there wasn't a Rugger match. Only today's really too hot for Rugger. I don't object to picnics as picnics you know. Only when you go to such infinite trouble for something that anyone with sense can do on the spot, it's not worth it in my opinion. And to make settled plans for one is worse than having to stay in a house. Just wander off is the best way in my opinion.

We wouldn't mind if we got a lift now: at present we are in a filthy mining village which is sure to smell like the devil (or worse, maybe the devil doesn't smell bad) when there's been hot weather for a week or so. Most places we are in will be decent in fine weather. But we can't have everything. Corporals Cameroon Berry and Professor Panting are discussing what they would do on a day like this at home. Program includes a girl in each case – odd men they are. We three intend (such is war <u>War</u> mind) to go for an evening into this town umpty miles back and have tea and perhaps our photos took and maybe a cinema. It's a funny war. We had the first aeroplane bombs I've seen some days ago. Don't often have them (thank Heaven) usually shells which you can hear coming: though personally I would rather not hear them coming because then if hit or hurt it's all over before you know – life would be dull without something to grouse about. You know that drowsy feeling when everyone just doses and thinks of nothing – well the heat's making everyone like that. It is queer having dust after so much mud, mud, mud.

Language from the doorway by Professor Panting – aeroplane annoying him by bussing in from behind a cloud. Has gone into the road to inspect it. Cameroon Berry also reduced to language. Completely fed up – only me left who hasn't 'given way'. Fine weather has a very soothing effect on me. Also another effect beginning with S meaning sleepy which I can't spell. My spelling (as doubtless you've discovered) not very strong. Have two of them looking for it. <u>Soporific</u> that's the word. Good.

John S. Riggs

23 March, 1916

Dear Dorothy,

Your letter came this morning just after I'd been told to attach meself to the 7th Batt. Leinster's 47th Brigade 16th Division.

Dorothy I'm really sorry now. I don't know what I said but I'm sure it wasn't nice. And I wish you would forget it. I've been rather wild the last fortnight or so because I'd been disappointed in not getting leave.

Yes, I'll tell you some of the books I've read. Only not just now because this is very rushed and I think I'll want something to do in the next month. So I'll try to remember some – will that do? Your explanation wasn't a waste of time. I'm afraid I did feel rather mad when writing last – not with you so much

– with myself and things in general. This is very rushed and I'll answer yours fuller later only. I want this to catch post out tonight. Write soon as I'll be writing in a day or two and I'll deserve one then.

John S. Riggs

P.S. Can you send me books, not mags as we can get them and they aren't much good.

27 March, 1916

Dear Dorothy,

This is being written in the trenches. I didn't expect to find myself here quite so soon but here I am. We've been here some days now and expect to have a worse time than we're having just now. After much trouble I have just succeded in getting a shave. This is quite an achievement let me tell you. Am really feeling quite clean considering I think I'll be with these people for a month, then I don't know what I'll do. Go back to my old job. I didn't intend to choke you off in that letter, only I expect I was feeling rather mad at the time and you came in for it. I'm sorry and please write at first chance as there's more excitement in getting letters here than when we were living further back. I've managed to bring up a couple of mags with me, and that's something when you have to carry everything up miles of trenches. I wonder did you ever read *In Search of Eldorado*? It's a yarn of two and sometimes four or five men who wander round. I'm writing under great difficulty as bits of mud are falling down my neck due to grenades landing. Another yarn that I liked tremendously was Rider Haggard's *Eric Brighteyes*. Maybe you've read it. I like these yarns – most of them more or less true – of old heroes, some of them were tremendous men, even when you deduct the usual amount of lies they tell. There isn't a lot to write about in this place. Or rather there is a lot but I don't want to write it.

I'm just after having a long yarn with a sergeant here who was working and studying the Belfast conditions in regard to Home Rule. Needless to say he became a strong home ruler and amongst the first things he said to me regarding Belfast Unionists was "they've no sense of humour". I'm afraid Dorothy that politics won't be much use after the war. And as for Civil War, well we won't want any more after the real thing.

It has started raining again – been fine for the last hour or two. I don't believe these trenches will ever get dry even in summer. This will go down with the ration party tomorrow. It's too late now for them to go this evening. It's dark now and the usual night game has started. Star shells etc. going off all the time. It's a great war. We have got a wee bit fire started, but as it has to be carefully concealed we get more smoke than heat. Still it's all in a life-time. We have got several Belfast men hereabouts, but chiefly Dublin way and the south. Altogether they are a most amusing lot and things are as cheerful as possible. I don't know why I keep on with this letter, I've nothing to say really and I just sit here and add a sentence now and again. Well I reely must say good night. Be as good as you can and why not wait till the Zeps come because then you might either steal it (?) from the shops in the confusion or get it cheap from the wreckage. Really I don't suppose you'll ever see one over there.

John S. Riggs

P.S. They gave me a rifle of course to bring along with me. Well that rifle is the curse of my existence. I've been used to a revolver which was easy. A rifle is a small cannon in comparison.

5 May, 1916

Dear Dorothy,

Your letter dated Monday came this morning. Really you know it is nice of you to write because I wasn't expecting one before I wrote, and I wasn't sure that the Postal Service was all right again. The letter I had from Mother yesterday was the first I've had from home since I came out again.

Four of us gentlemen have managed a bell tent between us. The rest of the company nowhere. In stables and shelters etc. of their own make. Well as it is fearfully hot weather it's very pleasant indeed and as we are in a wood and have electric light from the trench mains ("pinched" by me of course) we are

Despatch riders

quite home like. Baldrey, Berry, Panting and meself are the names in case you are interested. Nina would be I'm sure only she is awful hard to satisfy. Now I could recommend Berry to you if you could put up with his looks. Like a chicken Nina says and he's much hurt about it.

My dear girl!! My friends! Indeed. And are they the people Redmond stands for? Dorothy, pull yourself together! And yet and yet I do believe the devils believed (some of them) anyway that they were fighting for Ireland's glory. They were wrong of course and have paid with their lives. But it's a frightful pity that narrow minded people (like you Ulster unionists) will take it as representing Ireland. And when . . . Oh well it's no use talking with you but I've seen and been with the Irish out here and I know for myself (a man doesn't pretend under shell fire) what they think about Ireland and her freedom. Granted if you like it's sentiment and maybe difficult to work in practice, but can you deny the truth or glory of it all. You can't and that's where you people fail. Why even Sir Edward* (but he I'm sure didn't believe one half what he used to say about what are, after all his fellow countrymen) admits these Sinn Feiners don't represent any body of opinion. Well I for one am still a Home Ruler and I think Ireland has shown by her troops <u>here</u> that she is loyal to what's termed the Empire and which really stands for far more than country possessed.

I'm greatly amused by your being lenient with me. I wouldn't have been in the Dublin riots except to keep people from trouble, but if I had well I'm afraid I'd have wanted better friends than you to help me – so the lid would have been on, whatever that means. I'm sorry to keep on about politics but you were going to convince me in about two words I think when I was at home. Whereas I never heard a word about it. And as for your best arguments – why didn't you speak at all about anything let alone argue? Now I must admit I was disappointed about that, because I'm sure your reasons <u>must</u> have been good and new. I've heard most of the old ones fairly often and I'm afraid they don't hold water. And I can change my attitude about things – about once since the War anyway.

Honestly Dorothy leave was much as I thought and feared. With the exception of about three afternoons, the rest was failure and its not worth the journey. Well, it was in a way, but I was disappointed. And I know my family in one case did their little best to spoil one afternoon. But anyway don't you worry you have enough troubles by the time you are my age – I'm getting old rapidly. And why should I have too good an opinion of meself just because forsooth you were told by the servant that I might be your brother. <u>I'm</u> not worried and you've escaped!

I haven't read *A Man's Man* but the *Riddle of the Sands* I've read three times about three years ago . . . Really quite a good yarn and there are many things possible and I for one never even dreamed of war. I think Bruce Bairnsfather's foreword to his book in which he describes the new Kitchener army as "hating war as they hated Hell" is much the way I looked at it. And yet and yet – I've had dreams at times, but when I think it over on the moral side its all wrong.

*Carson

You know Ireland and everything seems such a long way off. And you've little or no future to look to. Oh well its just day to day and letters and books and things are all there is to remind you that there is another land and other lives better and more useful. Yes please I'd like to have the book. Only why make it such a point? You seem to take it as <u>such</u> a <u>serious</u> thing and I hate pretending that it is, because to me its not. I could get books sent direct only I'm too lazy. And again it costs money and I don't really like that. I don't want anyone's charity or their money. I wouldn't have any of their old tea or cakes or anything at the various stations because I want to pay for my own stuff and even if I paid I'd be under an obligation to you in some way, well I can't because you may not see it the way I do. I am heartily sorry if I've offended you but I don't suppose if I have its any use saying so. I must run now as I'm on night duty and two angry DO's will be waiting to be relieved.

John S. Riggs

Dorothy's mother, Jack, Rosemary, Dorothy and Archie

There must have been a very short leave at the end of March/early April. The following news-cutting is enclosed with the next letter:

Daily Express London, Friday 19 May, 1916:

Think Imperially

It is always the fate of the candid friend to be misunderstood. His advice, however well-intended, is nearly always unpalatable. Our plea that the present is a splendid opportunity for the peaceful settlement of the Irish question has brought on our heads torrents of wrath from the Ulster Press. We are "impertinent" to dare to offer counsel to our good friends of Belfast. We are traitors, and so on. At the same time – and this is a very significant fact – we have abundant evidence that we were speaking the mind of a large section of the English Unionist party . . . A portion of Ulster, unhappily, refuses to remember anything that has happened since the battle of the Boyne. Our offence is that we have suggested that the Boyne shall be forgotten, and that the nation shall endeavour to construct a happy tomorrow by bearing in mind the facts of yesterday and to-day. Great Britain must regard the Irish difficulty from the broad Imperial point of view. The Empire is more to us than the prejudices of County Antrim. From the Imperial standpoint the outstanding feature of the Sinn Fein revolt is that it was the work of a few fanatics, and that it was loathed and denounced by the immense majority of Irish Nationalists. Mr Redmond has stood emphatically for the Empire since the outbreak of the war. Nationalist Ireland stood emphatically by the Empire during the Sinn Fein week. These are the facts that seem to us to matter. It may please other people to recall the disaffection of the Boer war period. We prefer to remember the Irish soldiers of both parties heroically fighting now for the cause that is ours and theirs. It is true that Mr. Dillon's hectic speech in the House of Commons inevitably made compromise more difficult, but here again we venture to plead for an attempt at an understanding.

The Irishman is always on the side of the under-dog, provided that the dog is an Irish terrier. The Sinn Feiner in chains becomes a martyr to be avenged. It is easy to make martyrs in Ireland, and martyrs are the bitter enemies of statesmanship. We have, therefore, urged that a revolt which was a pitiful tragedy, for which the leaders were properly executed, should be followed, not by Prussian severity, but by wise conciliation. Sir Matthew Nathan's evidence before the Commission of Inquiry conclusively proves the hopeless incompetency of Dublin Castle. The Irish Government was warned, but it was afraid to act, and a Government that fears to do anything is utterly condemned. The men and women who died in the Dublin streets and the men who have since been executed are alike the victims of stupidity in high places. The Castle always suffered from the disadvantages that belong to alien rulers. The passing of the Home Rule Act, which automatically comes into operation at the end of the war, has caused it to fear its own shadow. Ireland has had no government at all, and the lawless have done exactly as they chose. This state of affairs cannot continue, and the only way out is to entrust Irish rule, at once, to Irish hands. The interests of Ulster received certain consideration in the Home Rule Act. That consideration, in Ulster's opinion and in ours, was entirely insufficient. We are convinced that if Ulster will now look facts in the face with the rest of Ireland and attempt to secure stable popular government she can ensure herself for ever from separation and from any chance of Nationalist tyranny. To effect this, however, Ulster must think Imperially. No one in England wants to "kick Ulster out". She is too valuable a portion of the State to be treated in such a fashion. But is Ireland for ever to be the battle-ground of faction and suspicion?

Editor's Note: *J. S. R. has scrawled at the bottom of the article "What other solution do you have? Because* <u>something</u> *must be done."*
David Trimble, one of the few sane voices of Unionism to emerge in the last quarter century, lost his seat in the recent General Election to the hard-line DUP candidate.

18 May, 1916

Dear Dorothy,
     Many thanks for your parcel. Came yesterday. And honestly I don't think that I deserve it. Because every time you do or offer to do anything I get wild. I can't explain why, only I always object at first. My native independence I suppose.
     My <u>friend</u> Cameroon Berry's features are <u>not</u> like your first, one of the others might be, only he's engaged already. We were just trying to find out from him some of his reasons, but he gave up his attempt at explanation in the middle.
     And I'm sorry in a way for the old rebels. By the way that's one point that I refuse to admit – that an Irishman can be morally accused of high treason. Because Ireland was a conquered country and those that raise these rebellions have never forgot it. And if you don't submit except to brute force how can you be disloyal when you've never professed loyalty. If we smashed Germany we couldn't accuse her people of high treason if they rebelled. And I believe that some of the brutes really thought they were helping Ireland. And country is a great thing at times. But I forgot, you don't have a country. You belong to the Empire in large letters don't you?
     My leave, thank you, was just what I expected. Except that you had led me to think that there would be an improvement, which there wasn't. And I'm not hard to amuse, really! Only when you spend at least half yur precious time doing nothing but doze or read in an armchair before the fire – well it's hardly life is it? Of course it's largely my own fault because I wouldn't exert myself to do anything else. And there wasn't anyone except Mr Lawrie? who was interested enough to come and see me and Mrs McIntyre. Anyway I wanted

to get out in the country or to the sea and enjoy life. I'm sorry if I gave the impression that I was bored at your place. I wasn't really. And I wish I could only have seen more people like yours. Anyway I did enjoy it. It was <u>one</u> of the afternoons you're so curious about. So there.

I quite looked forward to your arguments on Home Rule, because well <u>you</u> must mean them though the majority of Unionists do not. So I was interested to hear what they were. Anyway I'm afraid you wouldn't find me a very fine Home Ruler in spite of all I say. I admit that England in the latter years has been trying to help Ireland, but it shows with the best will in the world, she couldn't prevent the Dublin trouble, whereas I think Irishmen could, and it would be such a chance for your friends to show how they would run things when it came to real work not just play.

Two day interval: by the way I found this nice little news-cutting today. I think that it is fairly fair. I missed the post last night. You see it gets so infernally hot in the daytime that you can't write, and it's only at night that you can. Then it has to be rushed as the post goes at 7.20. Your books are passed on whenever anyone wants them, only you would be surprised at the number of people who wouldn't read anything except magazine stories. I've read your book. It is not (you'll get the truth) just the sort that I would sit up o'nights over, but it's worth reading and I'm grateful. But there's too much of the perfect hero touch in it. Most annoying these books are at times.

John S. Riggs

Jack reading in the garden of
Dorothy's house

There follows an unexplained gap until the letters resume:

25 July, 1916

Dear D.

I was most surprised <u>and</u> honoured to get your letter, but why such ambition to be rude? I thought you would be much more ladylike. The nice little French girls have been absent so far, but we are of course getting to know the country. We are moving again in a few days but this makes no difference to letters as they find us in time. As your mittens seem to be a drug in the market in spite of being so all round useful, and as I am very long suffering about clothing sent to me (ask Nina) they would very likely be useful as cleaning rags of which we are rather short.

Your remark about the grub is unfortunately only too true. We lived on bully beef and biscuits for about a fortnight but it has now improved to stew. I have sent S.O.S's to the family for milk etc. as none of these small things are supplied. The man who said they were well fed at the front! Well that's a polite letter. We are having rather an easy time after the last weeks in England. We used to be on duty all night & day there for 3 & 4 days on end. Now we have 4 hours on & 4 off which gives us a chance. We have seen several exciting events only I'll have to write these in a censored letter as this isn't.

These envelopes (Green marked On Active Service) are very scarce and we only get one a week. You will thus see how honoured you are. Course you mightn't feel so honoured if you knew that I have several. As I have supplied one letter from the front you might supply another from home. There are three of us at present living in a dug-out in a wood. Will write more fully later. Many thanks for your parcel.

John S. R

<u>Ed</u>. The above was written firmly with an italic-nibbed fountain pen in contrast to many earlier ones from the trenches which were in purplish-grey pencil.

12 September, 1916

Dear D.

I forget how long ago I last heard. I expect you have too. Well lots of things have happened. I've managed to come off a few times. Once, recently on my head. Of course I'm told I've been silly ever since, and that I'll never be quite the same again.

This is being continued 4 days later and there's no knowing when it will be sent. There have been quite a number of developments round this way & we expect to move soon. I remember now your last letter came when I was rather "bent" as you expressed it. And when that was better I broke a small bone, and when that was fit we were on the move for a fortnight or so. And then in action in a strange place which meant a lot of work. And now, well there's plenty doing. So it's not all my fault. I'm sorry I didn't write sooner, only you don't like P.C.'s

John S. Riggs

5 October, 1916

Dear Dorothy,

Well, I can't say I'm sorry because I'm not, but I can explain. You see Weaver used to write love letters for me but I complained that they weren't realistic enough and wanted better ones. So he said he'd write better if I gave him something to work on. And just then your letter turned up. As you wanted a letter I guessed that his would be much better than mine. I'm glad you're not very offended though I admit you have a right to be.

Nina says you have got madder than ever so it's no good accusing me, and she states that the only time you were serious was in the water. I'm so glad you have met Betty Joyce. If I remember her aright she wanted to <u>kiss</u> me the last time I met her. Really I'm surprised she didn't go as far with you. Holding hands doesn't count for much. I write my own letters except the ones you got. And that was your own fault as you said you preferred his. And Weaver is <u>quite</u> truthful to me anyway. This isn't very long but if you want any more letters from me <u>or</u> Weaver you say so. They have started shelling this place again & poor me must go to Y.O. with despatches. Ask Nina to explain Y.O.

John S. Riggs – the real one

30 October, 1916

Dear Dorothy,

Many thanks for your last letter – you seem to disbelieve me when I say I got hurt because I didn't tell the family. I don't tell the family things like that because mothers have silly habits. I would write my sisters only that goes through mother's hands I'm sure. I wonder if you know what it is to be writing to three or four people at once. It's annoying because you can't <u>really</u> write to one.

Berry has left us now as you may have heard. Why you got a card signed Berry, I don't know except maybe I asked him when my fist was bad – don't remember really. I'm honestly sorry I keep you waiting so long – only I didn't think you'd worry. You see I don't worry myself much when I don't get letters. Sometimes I'm weeks without when the post is held up – and why worry, if a letter is coming its coming & nothing you can do will alter it. And just why you thought I wasn't going to write <u>any</u> more I don't know. I'm afraid I often skip about a month before I write. It's a bad habit and one must pay for ones habits I suppose. <u>No</u> Miss Dorothy Kendall, I'm <u>not</u> fed up anymore than everyone here is, and I think myself that was rather a cheap sneer. Because there is plenty to be fed up about. Only I'm <u>not</u>. But I know I could be doing more useful work at home and it wasn't in my hands to settle it – I simply asked. I think if I'd asked earlier it might have been all right, but I'm quite content to stick here for the next year or two. Only it's such a fearful waste of time.

Anyway if you don't want to write again I'd like to thank you for what you have written and for the books etc. you sent. I won't say any more because I believe you would rather I didn't. But I am most grateful.

We are living at present in seas of mud. This was German trenches at one time and the ground is in an awful state. Smashed trenches & bits of houses and woods so shot away that you wouldn't believe one ever existed. Shell holes & barbed wire etc & no woods. Real fine life of it. We can't wash often because we can't get water – all that we get is used for cooking. A shell hole makes a good well at times if you can be sure there isn't anyone buried at the bottom. I hope you'll be able to forgive the delay in this letter. I honestly haven't the time and I hope you won't be too offended to answer. Just a P.C. if you are not wanting to continue, to say you've had this.

Yours sincerely, John S. Riggs

18 November, 1916

Dear Dorothy,

Your P.C. and letter received quite safely thank you. Of course I was very pleased to have your P.C. Such happiness to know that you were quite well – interval to shut the door here – everyone leaves it open. Well you are forgiven for thinking I wasn't writing any more. Only it wasn't quite without explanation. We moved quite some way and had a lot to do just then.

Yes, in a way I <u>am</u> fed up and so is everyone else out here. And its such an awful waste of time. Maybe you don't see it but I do. Leave is like everything else out here. Other ranks don't get any. Duty officers of course they need it after the "awful" hardships they have. I don't expect any myself this winter but maybe next summer or next winter if leave is still on I might get back. You must know that there are several men who haven't had any yet, and they don't stand any great chance either. I'm sorry to make you feel mean – there's no need to, because it was a lot to me and you can't claim that writing letters isn't a trouble to you. I know it is to me unless I happen to be in the mood, and then I really enjoy it. Strange, but 'tis so Dorothy. You seem to believe in the maxim of "Feed the Brute". Sort of "you can't go wrong" in that direction. Honestly I'm not asking for things when I write.

Yes I've read *Just So Stories*. It seems about 10 years ago though – it was only just before this b . . . war. My word! It seems quite like home to have crumbs in the bed clothes again. How about mice instead! We find them now & again in the blankets in the morning. Not rats, they aren't so loving. One gentleman had rather a nasty accident with one in his blanket – the poor mouse died – can you guess what happened?

19/ll/16

I got this far last night & then I had to go out, so I couldn't write again till now. I honestly thought you meant it that way and that you were not writing any more, I'm pleased that you aren't offended for ever. Though maybe you haven't really said what you think. If I'm too big a nuisance just say so. I feel that my letters must be an awful bore because I can't really write about anything, and you aren't that by any means.

John S. Riggs

11 December, 1916

Dear Dorothy,

Many thanks for your parcel – it was really very good and Cpl Harding wants to know what you flavoured the jam pies with as they tasted extremely well. We've moved from the last place & have now a front room in a town near here. We've got a real live fireplace & sofa & three armchairs & two beds & a table <u>&</u> curtains. As to your question about becoming one of the nuts – well I don't really want to. You see it's a matter of principle now, I'm not anxious because I didn't get the R.F.C. when I wanted it. Under the influence of your suggestion, however, I put my name down today when they asked for men to transfer to the tanks. They didn't mention giving commissions, but the captain thought it worthwhile to put my name down for one – I don't really want it though.

You see it's the justice of the arrangements about leave that trouble me. Not for myself so much. You may remember my opinions on that subject (may I say they've changed slightly?!) I always heard that you were not shy and were given to saying just what you wanted. And I thought that you would have so many others to write to who could write much nicer letters. I'm sorry about not asking. And how can I? So you've had another birthday. Just awful and in wartime too. It isn't too late to wish you many happy returns I hope. I'm sorry I couldn't send anything. It doesn't seem like a year since you sent that parcel. The cake was too good. I mean by this that it was gone *toute suite* sometimes (may I whisper? And don't on your life tell the family!) I get cakes which aren't in such a hurry to be eaten.

I would have answered sooner but I have to write several people at once so you had to wait till I had received a letter from mother I was waiting for. Sorry! I'll have to get that remark on a type stamp & sprinkle it about your letters in future. Save a lot of time. I'm nothing if not workmanlike. Well I hope you realise it's your fault if they make me a general or something. And I wasn't really grousing about leave. I'm afraid if the home people really heard the grouses about the war, it would open their eyes a bit.

John S. Riggs

28 December, 1916

Dear Dorothy,

I had your last letter just before Xmas and I'm writing just as I've recovered from the exertions of the day.

Cpl. Harding for his sins is a cold Englishman. He has also the misfortune of being my fellow D.R.S.[?] I sometimes use his soap etc. Of course we haven't been introduced, but it's "wartime you know & one must put up with this class of people". We got something to put in the fireplace all right. Two D.R.S.s took a sidecar round to the coal dump and one was a s'nofficer who talked to the sergeant in charge who filled (with his own sweet hands) our sack. The s'nofficer then rode off sitting on top of the sack in the sidecar and the D.R.S. arrived at our billet with coal. Sinful isn't it? And do you really think that 2nd Lieuts are listened to in the matter of leave.

I'm wondering whether to take your "not worrying about grammar or proper words" as a compliment or not. It's maybe a back-handed one. I believe I'm flattered anyway. I've looked up "bumptious" in the Dic. It only gives bumphism "a clumsy rustic". Now just what do you mean by that and when & what way? ("In answering please number your sheets & write only on one side"). Surely you wouldn't wear any blouse so out of date as that will be when I get leave. I'd always been taught to regard you as a most fashionable young lady!

I don't suppose you really want my opinion of peace. You must remember that anybody's opinion who's in the mud is liable to be peace at any price. But honestly it has quite heartened most of the boys. We all want it bad and you must think that a lot of lives are going to be lost if we go in. For all that I don't think we'd welcome peace just now. Say next autumn when Fritz has got something of what's coming him. He got <u>some here</u> last autumn & I guess there will be more.

The family can tell you whereabouts I am. At least they can tell you a town behind the line that I've visited. It's some distance back and they don't charge for things oh no! The people here seem far more after the cash than up north. It's the Australians who did a lot of that – they didn't care what they gave as long as they got it.

I've seen several of your friends the tanks. Nice beasts. Myself & the artificer here (who came up specially for the tank) spent half an hour inspecting one in front of a brigade officer of ours. I think I'd enjoy them myself.

I don't know if I mentioned last time that we went to see the Battle of the Somme on the film last place we were in. And after enduring about 3 hours of awful film they didn't show it. Most disappointed – we had quite hoped to see ourselves. There was a film at the time of the [?] Martin push through and he took a lot of the chaps. Maybe you've seen the film.

Of course this last place was when we were in rest – we can't have these little pleasures here. We are sleeping (you can <u>just</u> call it that) in a tent without any boards. It is fine when it rains or freezes and two or three inches of mud is on the floor. We've got what we call beds. A wooden framework with wire netting on legs: this keeps us out of the mud and you feel quite like home once you're in bed. It's one of my last pleasures that the army has left me. Going to bed.

This commission job stops all chance of leave of course. They reckon I suppose that you live in hopes, Which I don't. I chucked it last time for leave at once. And I doubt now if it was worth it. Again leave takes a longer journey here about two days I believe to reach home. Awful in French trains. Bad enough when it was 12 hours. They gave us two green envelopes at max. – kind wasn't it? And you were informed that the latest you could part for home was the 17th.

I'm certain the Russian head dress will add to the effect of the dance. People will think it's intended to be that way. And even if they don't what matter? A small thing like that you'll surely be able to bluff it out all right.

Don't forget to see what your dictionary says about bumptious – most interested!

John S. Riggs

1917

The first letter from Jack is dated 14 March, Dorothy's diary entry for Sunday 17 February, 1918 says: "Exactly a year today since Jack came home. He came with Nina just after tea on the Saturday evening – I'd been in bed with a cold, and had just got up. They left early – after asking me to go down there on Sunday the 18th."

    The following entries cover the home leave period Monday, 18 February to Tuesday, 12 March, 1917:

Monday 18: Just a year ago today I spent the afternoon and evening at the Bank (Ulster Bank, Waring Street, Belfast). Jack came home with me and stayed to supper

Wednesday 20: A year ago Jack came about 4.30 & we talked with a few pauses for breath till supper time. After some persuasion he stayed. We arranged to go to the Tank film on Friday.

Thursday 21: A year ago – Class at Central Hall (Dancing). Nina came in the middle of it to ask if I could go to the pictures that evening instead of Friday. I went home and changed and then called at the Bank about 7. We all (Jack, Ledlie, Myra and me) went to the Imperial to see the Tanks. Myra went home early with her father. Jack wanted to take me home but I sent him back with Ledlie as it wasn't at all late. Slight 'camelious hump' at this!

Friday 22: A year ago – errands in the morning. Town in the afternoon. Went to Bank, found Nina in bed – took her some books. Met Daddy about 5 and went to D.I.M.A. to see Mr Couch – signed on for munitions. Didn't see Jack today.

Saturday 23: A year ago – Errands, sewing, walk with Rosemary. Just before tea Jack and Gertie came to ask me to go to a footer match with him the next day – they didn't stay long.

Tuesday 26: A year ago – Jack was at Dublin seeing Vera so I didn't see him. Rained most of the day – pretty dull.

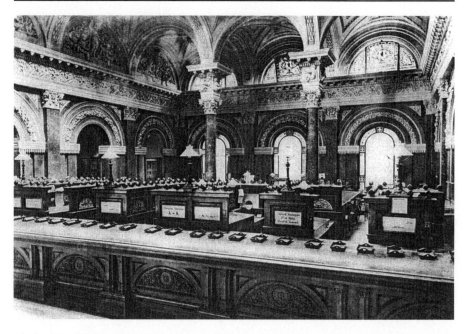

The banking hall in Waring Street taken at the time of opening in 1860. Note the wide counter and the rows of trays used to push cheques and lodgements etc across it.

Wednesday 27: <u>A year ago</u> – Went and got stuff for my dress as 'Snow Queen'. Jack came for tea. BSH called just as tea was over to tell me about a rehearsal – talking, music and chess all evening.

Thursday 28: <u>A year ago</u> – Dancing class & rehearsal in the afternoon. Went with Jack and Ledlie to the "Little Minister" at the Opera House in the evening. I came home alone as Jack took Ledlie back.

Friday 1: <u>A year ago</u> – Walk with Rosemary in the afternoon – Jack came with Charlie's car about 5 to ask me to go for a run the next day – stayed for tea and a short time after. Wet evening. He took me to "On the Stairs" rehearsal at Richmond Lodge [*Dorothy's school*] via Marlborough Park. Sat in the car at the gate till it was time for me to go in.

Saturday 2: Just the same sort of day as last year when Jack and I went in Charlie's car down to Larne via Ballyclare and back by the coast road.

Sunday 3: <u>A year ago</u> – Went up to Osborne Park to see Jack play Rugger. The other team were very late in arriving so Jack, I and Mr Laurie talked till Gertie came. They began to play soon after she arrived. Great fun but very cold and wet while watching. Gertie and I waited afterwards till Jack had changed & we went down on the tram together. They wouldn't come to tea so I left them and came home myself.

Exterior of the main building iin Waring Street

Monday 4: <u>A year ago</u> – Cold wet day. Went down to the Bank after dinner and cut out Ledlie's Ice Maiden dress for her – had a game of chess with Jack – tea – Mr Laurie was there. Impromptu game of Rugger round the passage – ping pong. Bill came in to speak to Jack. Came home about 8.30 – Jack came with me and stayed to supper.

Tuesday 5: <u>A year ago</u> – Went with BSH to see Mrs Kernaghan about her dress (Granma in the Snow Queen). Very cold and snowy. Didn't see Jack today.

Wednesday 6: <u>A year ago</u> – Dancing class and rehearsal in the afternoon. Came home and changed – collected Jack and Gertie at the Bank and went to *Niobe* – very amusing. Missed tram so left Gertie home & then Jack came up as far as Adelaide Park – he walked to the gate with me but didn't come in. We arranged to meet in town the next day and have tea somewhere.

Friday 8: <u>A year ago</u> – Went down town & met Jack at 12 o'clock. We went to the Savoy together – talked about many things. Came home about 1.15 after arranging for him to come to tea the next day. Old girls meeting in the evening. Reading of *As You Like It* – I took the part of the old duke.

Saturday 9: <u>A year ago</u> – Jack came in the afternoon and helped me with the roof of the doll's house. After tea played chess and talked muchly. Arranged to go to the match tomorrow at Osborne.

Sunday 10: <u>A year ago</u> – Jack came about 2.50 and took me up to see a match at Osborne Park. Inst. and some officers' scratch team. Home for tea. Chess and talk after tea till supper time. Arranged to go for run in motor on Monday.

Monday 11: <u>A year ago</u> – Dull, cold day got several photos taken in my fancy dress. Read and worked at doll's house.

Tuesday 12: <u>A year ago</u> – Jack came at 3 o'clock & took me out in the wee car. We got a puncture about St John's school. Mended it and went to Hillsborough via Shaw's Bridge, Ballyauchlis, Dumbo hill and Lisburn – back via main road. Got chocs at Rigby's & home to tea about 6 o'clock. Chess, talk etc. all evening – Jack left at about 10.35. He was going the next day to England to report at Dunstable.

14 March, 1917

Dear Dorothy,

I've arrived in this spot. Dunstable – nice place. Only I didn't think so. I got here about 11 a.m. & hoping to be out of it again before night. I went up and reported straight away, only to be told that there weren't any orders for me & of course nobody can say when there are likely to come. I was in a vile temper. Oh yes I was. Just kicking myself for coming. But that was my sense of duty. Anyway about tea time I found another man in the same fix which consoled me somewhat. Queer isn't it when there is anyone to grouse to how it passes over. Then I had a really rotten half hour or so. Just lonely you know. I am like that at times. So I rushed off & sent a telegram. Felt better then also met the D.R., I came over with who had got his orders very late and was a day late. So we went and had tea and then went to the pictures. By the way the <u>official</u> feeding is <u>I think</u> awful, but of course you can always get a square meal. My tummy is a very important part of me as you know.

I'm writing this in bed. Yes I have a bed. I saw Vera on Tuesday evening, and she came down to the boat with me. I'll tell you what was said later. I <u>didn't</u> tell her about you quite, though she <u>did</u> ask. This is just a note so that you all owe me one. Its mean I know; but I want to hear soon. If I leave hurriedly I'll wire again. In any case these people will forward to me. Suddenly struck me if you can read this. Try anyway & tell me if you can't. I'll see what can be done then. More later.

Good night. J. S. Riggs

Cadet John S. Riggs 41952,
R.A. Cadet School, Trowbridge, Wiltshire
18 March, 1917

Dear Dorothy,

I haven't heard from you yet, but you have been good at some time or other, so I'll just write again. As I wired you I'm at Trowbridge now. I haven't done any work yet – that starts on Monday. I understand it is a 12 weeks course here. Did Nina say anything to you about coming over here for 10 days or so in the summer? Don't say anything to her if she hasn't, but she suggested it to me. And of course someone was to come with her either you or Barbara or both! I don't know if you would come supposing she was serious about it. I had a letter from her & Mother today – seems Mother has sent my kit to Dunstable! I don't know how I'll get it now. Doesn't matter very much except that I'll have to pay for it and I'm awful "Jewish" now. Dorothy aren't parents a nuisance sometimes? Maybe if you . . . no I won't say that because it's not time really.

About Vera. She asked about you and I told her we were very good chums. She wanted to know if you knew I liked you, and when I said yes she also thought it wasn't fair to you. So now, Miss there are people who agree with me on that point. Do you really think it is yourself? I'm afraid I don't worry much if it is or not <u>now</u>. You needn't say anything to the family as I haven't told them in case it doesn't come off, but I believe we get four days at the end of this month. I'll do my little best to get over even for a day. Might just as well travel as stay here by myself or go to London. I hope Miss Kendall won't be on ammunitions by then. Could you get away if she was do you think? I expect that it will be the only leave I'll get when I'm here.

Dorothy can't you get a copy of the photo of you that Nina had on her mantlepiece in the Bank? The room I slept in it was, when you were still a flapper I think, but it was very like you.

The soldiering here is fierce at present. They are trying their very hardest to make me an officer <u>and</u> a gentleman – they might make me an officer. Little doubt about the other. Even you didn't really succeed did you? You know I don't really like the English much, and as for the girls – well. Of course you have had the tremendous advantage of living in Ireland which has improved you. Made you almost (but not quite) perfect. Maybe in return for your great kindness to me I'll point out one or two little details that want rounding off so to speak. The inane giggle for instance – I must admit it vanished a lot and I take full credit for that! Silly kid.

I really must write three or four more letters and you will be doing what your mother said I would "getting too good an opinion of yourself". I don't think I'm likely to do that myself because I can never believe things that way. I know what you said when I told you I didn't see why you put up with me. Dorothy I'm afraid I'm built that way that unless I do something for people I can't believe they are interested. It's just I recognise the selfishness in people & myself. I wanted to explain this because you said I was 'fishing' at one time. Well I wasn't girl. I don't quite believe it yet. You only saw me on leave and I was always (now wasn't I?) good tempered. You always think better of people you don't see too much of because you don't see their faults so easy or you must see everything about them & forgive it recognising your own. Sorry, but I get that way at times – that's what your mother & I would discuss. Not you. You're only the child yet! Really must stop girl.

John S. Riggs

P.S. Well what sort of a time did the family give you after I left: Very bad.

Studio portrait

Trowbridge 21 March, 1917

Dear Dorothy,

Your letter dated 17 March came on the 19th. I couldn't answer it at once & owing to an outbreak of measles in Trowbridge I couldn't yesterday. This may seem odd, but hist fair maiden & I'll explain.

You see most of the men hire rooms to work in during the evening. I think myself it's chiefly love letter writing, but let that pass – work in sounds so much better. Besides we do a little at times. Well owing to these measles the rooms of most of them are out of bounds as is Trowbridge itself, all shops etc. Today we discovered that our room isn't as it isn't classed as yet as in the town. All of my writing material & papers etc. were here so I couldn't write or get them and we couldn't buy anything. Sad isn't it?

The shamrock I'm sorry to say didn't turn up till yesterday. I bought mine in London where I stayed the night (saw *The Bing Girls are Here*). Rotten in my opinion. Of course it's the company that really makes these entertainments for me anyway. I have not been here before. Salisbury Plain is just south I believe and we were on the southern limit of the plain almost. The country round here is quite decent but one really wants a motor to do much good. And that can't be did in England. I forget who the D.R. was. I do really. My dear girl if you adopt that patronising tone about men & their meals I'll shake you next time.

Girl, I don't think I have to tell you about Vera. I won't more than is necessary because it's not very nice. I'm not pleased to hear you are in disgrace – this is serious. I never thought your mother would think that. Dorothy you know I don't think that you played with me. Don't be a silly girl. But why can't you explain? I don't know of course what she said. I'm going to write her anyway and point out what a difference you made to my leave. Maybe she'll see from that. Dorothy I could kick meself I just hate to think I've made you quarrel with your mother. You seemed such friends to me (your mother I mean). Dear girl you were more than fair to me – I can't yet believe how good you were.

I don't think you need worry about outsiders because you didn't do anything so very dreadful. I mean anytime or anything we did, well surely even your mother knows, it was at my suggestion.

I wonder Dorothy would you do one small thing for me. I'd ask the family (don't tell them this) but I don't trust them after the kit bag trouble. And your father could help if he would. I'll need, in a fortnight or so a 10 inch slide-rule: there is a shortage I believe and you have to order. Would you see if you could get one in Belfast? Your father could tell you where. Don't get it of course. Just see. About 15/- is usually the price I think. I had a small one, only I sold it before the war. I'll send whatever it is. Seems silly maybe but I don't want to have to order & maybe wait a month or so before I get it.

I'll write to your mother now.

John S. Riggs – Cadet

Trowbridge – 25 March, 1917

Dear Dorothy,

I had yours of the 20th on Thursday or Friday – not sure which. I wasn't in an awful hurry to answer because there was one of mine on the road which should be enough for you. And you would get bored if you got too many! Maybe you wouldn't value them enough! You needn't think this is <u>any</u> excuse for not writing at any time because it isn't.

Your shamrock arrived but I didn't find any note I'm sorry to say. I looked too because I half expected one. ("Conceit" I can hear you say). The course will be the only one before commission – that is if ever I get it – there are more to be done after, but that's different. I hope with luck to be home on Friday morning which means that unless you are down town in the morning I'll see you I hope on Friday afternoon. I will then try to answer any odd questions that escape in this letter.

I'm sorry about the summer in England trip. I thought it was too much to hope for myself. There are limits to luck unfortunately. I am sorry (not <u>very</u> really – it might do you good) that you had such a lot of chaff. My honest opinion is that you rather enjoy it, because I'm sure you get your own back. You don't seem a person to be easily put upon somehow. Nina didn't send any messages. Said you had been in & that she had a dreadful time with you.

What I was going to say wasn't anything very important. It was that maybe if you hadn't driven? your mother away that evening she wouldn't have stopped when I took so long starting up and I don't do it to annoy. Its – well if I was talking you would guess or it wouldn't be necessary to say more. I forget in letters that the tone of voice isn't there & that you won't guess. No I haven't got to know <u>any</u> while I've been here and don't want to. They don't look nice you know.

I certainly don't hold a poor opinion of you – you know that. I didn't mean I didn't believe it – though that's what I may have said – just that it seemed unbelievable. But I don't think it was for what I could do, because I can't do anything.

Bed time. Bugle just gone. I'll talk to you about things when I see you. You'll hardly have time to write before I get away. Till then bear up.

Yours John S. Riggs

Trowbridge, 27 March, 1917

Dear Dorothy,

This won't be very long, as it is nearly time I was in bed, and you know I wouldn't miss me bed even for the pleasure of writing to you!

I'm sorry I gave you so much trouble about the slide rule. I thought maybe that even though there was a shortage, Belfast being an out of the way spot might be able to produce one. I'll order one in London or get someone going there to get one for me. In the meantime I'd be very grateful if your father would lend me one till my own turns up. I'll see you and him anyway about it. The Rugger between Inst & Campbell was I thought excellent. No but honestly you have learned. Of course look what tuition you had! I've told the family & your mother that I'll likely be home on Friday. We have been told so anyway so that is enough to go on.

I don't want to see France again – at least in some ways. If things happened often enough it would be different, but anyway girl it's been worth it to me. I'm not having <u>such</u> an awful time here of course. I've started this and can't quite finish & and if I don't you'll be cross – I can't quite express it – anyway I bet you can guess pretty well.

Yours John S. Riggs

Trowbridge, 27 March, 1917

Dear Mrs Kendall,

I wasn't bored or anything like that by your letter, I liked it awfully. I must confess it was rather a strange letter to me. I'd never had any quite like it before.

It came with Dorothy's yesterday. I hope with luck to be home for a day or two on Friday. Maybe this may not come off at the last minute, but that is the arrangement at present. Billet we are in is a large warehouse which has been converted into barracks. We are quite well off. They even give you warm water to wash in the morning & for baths. And the feeding though rather short is really good and quite enough to live on.

It was just because you did let me come in and out when I liked as if it was my home, that my leave was so enjoyable. You may not see it but it did make all the difference to me. When the Bank got me "fed up" I could just clear out & I <u>did</u> enjoy going to you. I'm not at all used to being "forward" as you put it but I don't know. I used to wish sometimes – but somehow it never did happen that way – and I'm afraid I've dried up now & grown old. Because I have grown awfully old in some ways, and in others, well I notice it even here amongst the other men, that my pleasures etc. are far nearer the schoolboy than men. I don't think I will alter that. I don't want to. And don't please try to make letters "interesting" it would spoil them if I thought you were writing with that idea. I'd rather you wrote as your last. About your cutting: it is of course written about an infantry cadet school where they haven't so much to do. Otherwise it is quite a good picture. We have a few (very few) men who are not B.E.F. and it makes a difference. Will you believe that in spite of the thieving that we have been used to in France you could and can leave anything about here and find it again?

I hope I'll see you before the end of the week with luck (always put that in to keep off bad luck). So I won't write more just now.

John S. Riggs

Dorothy's diary for Saturday 30 March, 1918:

A Year Ago – Jack came home on week-end leave from Trowbridge. Arrived up here about 4 o'clock & stayed till about 10.30. Arranged to go to footer match tomorrow – very cold and wet.

Sunday 30: A Year Ago – Met Jack at Gibson's corner about 2.40 – went to Ormeau to match between R.B.A.I. and Dungannon. Inst won. Walked across to University Road through snow. Snowed all evening. Chess, talk after tea. Jack went home about 10.30.

Monday 1: A Year Ago – Went down to the Bank in the afternoon. Jack was in with Nina when I arrived and didn't come into the drawing room for some time as he didn't know I was there. Chess etc. till tea time. After tea went and saw his motor bikes in the shed in the yard. Then ping-pong till it was time to come home – he came up with me. Snowy evening. Had supper and talk here.

Tuesday 2: A Year Ago – Jack came early about 3.15 & we talked etc. all afternoon. Had tea promptly & he left soon after as he was crossing back to Trowbridge that night by Fleetwood – snowing when he left.

Trowbridge, 5 April, 1917

Dear Dorothy,
   Life is still worrying on here. First it snows & then rains & then is quite warm. Still it's better than France. The other two men are being good little boys & doing "buzzer" – know what that means? Just morse on the instrument. They are both better than I am but I have no patience with the thing & won't do it. Not tonight anyway. Something better to do!
   Decent of you to write so soon. You <u>can</u> be a good girl when you like I believe – my influence of course. So you can set this off against the other portion, though somehow I can't see you doing the other if you didn't want to. (She always assured me that she wouldn't do things just because they pleased <u>me</u> anyway!)
   I didn't forget the slide rule: and little girls shouldn't be impertinent to their elders. Also the R.T.O. was as I thought quite helpless and couldn't say one way or the other. So of course I went & it was quite all right. You seem awfully afraid of spoiling me or making me too conceited. Now why? Am I so easily spoiled or made conceited?
   I rather like the idea of the haughty Miss Kendall freezing upstairs. Must be so good for her! But really girl it was decent to write so soon. I wasn't exactly "down" but I certainly wasn't too happy. It's one blessing about this place that you haven't too much time to think or start wanting things. And I'm quite sure that you don't often indulge in a howl. Surely surely you're much too grown up for that. Remember its only very little girls that do that sort of thing. Besides

how bad for the eyes. You might wash some of the colour out or even change it. I guess you'll think this is a silly letter. I know this is fearful paper. I had to get some & this was all that could be got in the time. I did want to write you tonight. [*He is using the same stiff cream coloured paper as before: from the trenches it was much lighter weight and written in pencil rather than ink. Ed.*] The other two men are off to bed and I must follow soon.

Oh, I forgot. Yesterday I had a letter from Vera who <u>was</u> at home all the time it seems, telling me she was. When she wrote it was a week ago & its only just got here after I'd been home & back again. She was expecting me to go & see her when I did come. I expect she will be crazy with me. I'll try & bear up. By the way was there anything <u>wrong</u> with your costume in the Ballet? Satisfy you alright?

This isn't the sort of letter I was going to write, but it will have to do now. I'll write the other another time. Do you think if I got a chess board & men here we could do any good?

John S. Riggs

Trowbridge, Thursday 12 April, 1917

Dear Dorothy,

I am sorry about the letter card. I knew you would hate it. I do meself and look upon them as a crime, but I hadn't any stamps and a "gentleman" offered me one so I used it. I think I mentioned it was the first I'd used. Your letter came yesterday & would have been answered last night only we have just got deep into a torture called "B.C. Corrections" which kept me busy. They will also shorten this and I don't hope for a chance to write to you before the week end. <u>Can</u> you possibly bear up till then?

As I told you we have only a couple of hours free in the evenings and it just flys when you are working at interesting things. So maybe she'll let me off lightly this time. I haven't read "Etcetra" yet but will certainly do so as soon as I can get it & time. I can't afford to waste time now – my conscience you know.

I can see from the second part that you were really getting cross because you thought I didn't write. Maybe I was too. But I am older of course & realise that these things can't always be as we want them and I'm afraid she must have a guilty mind if she thinks I would get cross & refuse to write. I think I should rush into ink at once if she did make me really cross. Anyway I'm not capable of giving you a real good slanging I'm afraid. I quite agree it would do you good but what can one say to a child? Pleased to hear about your tooth. I didn't know you objected to being called girl. <u>What</u> are you then? I don't look upon it as any punishment to be called anything. I have been called much worse things and still live. Only I'm afraid I'm not a boy any more. Worse luck. Oh I don't mean I'm growing up or wise or anything insulting to you, but I can't be so carelessly happy as I used to.

This takes me to your third sheet. I'll answer that later. You are a dear girl to write so much for me. I wish I could return it only as I have often said I can't write letters. And why you kept writing me when I was in France is still a wonder to me. You wrote such nice jolly letters. And they did help. It _is_ worth while when there are people like you. Even at the finish, I'm afraid I'm always getting serious with you and I wonder sometimes do you see it & understand, or just laugh to pass it. I really must run Dorothy – you are a terrible person to get away from.

John S. Riggs

Trowbridge, Sunday 15 April, 1917

Dear Dorothy,

It seems ages since I wrote to you last, and it isn't really long. I've had quite a lot to do the last few days & the news from France has been so great, and there have been such changes in the time table here that it makes it seem long since I wrote. We now start work before breakfast – this is a perfectly horrid idea. How can one manage to <u>think</u> on an empty tum? I can't anyway. I don't know what will happen when we are tested in "buzzer" and I can't say I've ever noticed the "respectfully" part about <u>you</u>. Also bet you never felt it!

I think I can be patient when I'm interested in anything. I am slightly in you. Rather an interesting study you make. England's Young Idea (and how silly it can be). As for trying your best to annoy me. I know you haven't as yet anyway, at least you always climb down if you think I am. I quite admit you try to be insulting etc. but we both are so that doesn't count. You'll be pleased to hear I've got a slide rule of my own now. I could send yours back now but as I don't suppose you are in a vast hurry I'll just keep it till I finish. I think you'll find everything on a slide rule is simple, the idea being to remember how to do it. Now if I tell you why I asked about your dress at the Ballet don't ask anymore. I was <u>told</u> it wasn't right. I didn't believe it (that _is_ a compliment) but I thought maybe something had gone wrong. I knew of course that as you intended it, it would be perfect! I am sorry to hear you're in bed, but as you didn't grouse and seem rather proud of being there, and there are worse places, I won't waste any sorrow. I only hope your eyes won't be too "blinky" to read this.

When you put (after a French word) "that's French" is it to reassure yourself or to enlighten me? Weather has been slowly getting better here & then breaking again. Now it's like summer. I hope to explore round here although I'm afraid it will be limited, after the first exam which will be in another fortnight. One of the <u>gentlemen</u> I room with is on guard. The cadets do it at week ends which amounts to about once each during your time here, and the other is here writing notes. Not this sort of note. All about ropes & tackle etc. "<u>Very</u> interesting" I can hear you say. I suppose you will be on munitions next time I'm home. And you are sure to be much too tired & cross to live with in the evening. I'll try it though. If you get too bad you'll have to be sent to bed. That will give me a hold over you because I'm sure your mother will agree. So she'll have to try to be good – it won't be Dorothy though if she is. Pause here while I dipped into G.A.T. Vol. III (Garrison Artillery Training). I think this is enough for one letter and I must write home and then notes.

John S. Riggs

21 April, 1917

Dear Girl,

There's been a long pause between the last and this. While I consider <u>you</u>. I get taken with fits of what shall I call it, sadness, sorrow and doubt which are rotten while they last. And somehow I want <u>you</u> to fix it. Just writing you is the best I can do and that does help. But it would take you in person to really finish it.

You'll not enjoy this letter anyway I'm afraid dear. I feel oh just rotten – about nothing really except what very little we do and get. I mean that for months of work & trouble (work should be & is often a pleasure) we get about two or three hours happiness. It doesn't seem right and yet its heaps more than some people have. That is what keeps me from grousing. Thinking how much less one might have had. I often envy the older men because they have had their time in peace. I wonder if you hate this. I do usually myself because you can't afford to think like that. But sometimes I give way because there seems so little to look forward to and work for. And it's such a short life that the waste of time worries me & I get downhearted. I would like to talk to you <u>now</u>. Maybe it wouldn't be all talk though. *Enfant!* You know I told you I never dared to hope for anything good in the future. Well that was chiefly in France of course, but I am always afraid to expect too much from the future because it may not come, and if it does I may be disappointed. I am like a child in that I hate, oh hate, to be disappointed. Now well I <u>dare to hope</u> that there's some happiness somewhere in the future & to count on it. But always I'm afraid. I am a coward you see. It <u>is</u> a cowardly way to go about but I'm afraid the time in France is accountable for a lot. I have never, not to anyone, till now admitted that to me the worst part was to be there with so little to look for in the end. And I'm afraid I got savage with things. And yet well I'm not sorry, because I was with some tremendous men. To be with them was an honour I never felt worthy of somehow. Maybe you can understand a little Dorothy, and I don't really feel like this often you know. Only I want to tell her for warning. Dear girl I shouldn't worry you like this. It isn't playing the game I think to put grouses on paper. Because for instance I've quite cheered up now but the grouses remain for you. And you can't be expected to know how much or how little I mean.

Oh – about your different types of writing. Why not say red ink for anger, black for being serious and pencil when you are silly. You will notice that as you usually write in pencil it won't mean much extra strain on you.

I can be <u>quite happy</u> you know sometimes. But it is so hard to realise it at the moment. Because you doubt somebody at the time. Afterwards it's over.

I haven't really finished but am posting this tonight.

John S. Riggs

22 April, 1917

Dear Dorothy,

Writing again on Sunday. I wish now I hadn't posted last night's letter. Because I'm sure to have said the wildest things that will only worry you. That's if you ever are worried which I doubt. You always seem so cheerful.

I was at a concert here on Friday. Feeble in the extreme, I came away after half an hour. One dame who sang (fearful voice) had a face it was painful to look at. Oh, so you don't think we have spring cleaning. Let me tell you Miss that we have it every morning. We don't of course have to do it all ourselves, but it is done every morning. Your idea of a Strafe never does get beyond an idea because then you are reminded that a perfect lady does not do these things. So I am quite safe except from your tongue & I'm not frightened of <u>that</u>. I hope of course that my rudeness won't get worse, after all the trouble you have taken that would be a poor result. Only I thought I might be allowed to be at least as rude as you try to be. You must admit you do try hard at times. Still I should worry.

All sorts of things come into Artillery and Engineer work – you have to lift things even ashore sometimes. Didn't that occur to you? Must attend to the fire here: the other two gentlemen are sleeping in front of it. Effects of eating too much dinner! Suddenly we always get a little more because there are a good few away at week ends. There doesn't seem anything I can get into words to say to you. You are such an irresponsible sort of person that I'm surprised you wish for things at all. Yes, I want my next leave all right. Only then I won't realise what I have till I'm going again. Chiefly I think because everyone takes it as a matter of course and it isn't to me. Seems wonderful to have nearly all you want. I am writing awful nonsense just for the sake of writing you. Please girl don't hold me responsible for everything I've said because I often couldn't tell you what I have said. You'll say, I know, that I should have a carbon copy & refer back to it when I get yours in answer.

What are we going to do next time I come back. You'll be on munitions I suppose. And that doesn't leave much does it? And I suppose the old car will be away. It should be about June sometime with any luck at all.

This might I think finish – there hasn't been much in it. Just a ramble on about nothing. How do <u>you</u> manage to keep awake. You must have a guilty feeling or you wouldn't suggest that I fall asleep. You know I feel such a useless animal and at other times I'm so careless that it doesn't seem to matter. This is all nonsense. Don't heed these last letters except that I have written and you'll write.

John S. Riggs

30 April, 1917

Dear Girl,

Do you know I made five attempts to write you yesterday & tore up each one. Somehow I couldn't write even you yesterday. There isn't a great deal of news: weather has become very hot & I find work very tiring. Yes work – I do sometimes but only if I'm driven to it. Will you count this as a letter as I don't know quite when I'll get writing again. I succeeded in passing the "Matériel" exam that we have at the end of the first six weeks. Now we forget all about it and start afresh. You do talk such solid sense in your letters sometimes. I mean this – your last letter wasn't a "let down" at all. On the contrary I was quite contented. I picked up a yarn here called *Adventures of a D.R.* which I got to criticise but found it almost exactly what the life of a D.R. at Divisional HQ was like. Of course the man who wrote it went out early & things being on a smaller scale they moved faster. Otherwise it is what the job was like. I don't know if you'll like it. You needn't read it of course if you aren't interested and some of it will be dull I guess. Anyway I think I'll risk sending it.

John S. Riggs

Letter card Trowbridge – 3 May, 1917

Dear Girl,

I can't write you tonight. Really you know I <u>am</u> afraid of you. Why I don't know you may think I diagnose it rather well. This place needless to say doesn't seem very cheerful just now. Very few of the other men are back yet though it's 10 p.m. I had quite a nice journey though troubled with hunger as they have been inconsiderate enough to take the dining cars off the trains. Been quite a lot of snow here too it seems.

So old America has come in at last! That's what is about here anyway. First time I used one of these vile things – hope it will be the last.

John S. Riggs

4 May, 1917

Dear Dorothy,

I guess there won't be a great deal of interest in this, but I have a few moments, and they couldn't be better occupied than in writing to you could they? About our spring cleaning you are so doubtful about. Well <u>we</u> don't do it but the orderlies are supposed to. Yes, I guess the house you would manage would be rather a joyous affair. [*From Dorothy's diaries it is clear that, despite the family having a domestic servant, she was expected to do quite a lot of house cleaning and that she loathed it.*] Now you can take any meaning you like from that, so you can't blame me.

You may remember a yarn I mentioned I might send you about a D.R. Well on second thoughts I won't. You might put it down to conceit on my part. But I honestly don't think you would find it "worthwhile" reading. I did, but it's different to me. I divide most reading into two sections those "worthwhile" & those not. Of course the worthwhile vary from the just worthwhile to things you really should read. I mean "worthwhile" to spend the time in reading. Because though I read a lot of all kinds of stuff I have a feeling that it is a waste of time. I know of course that in some cases it isn't and you get the considered opinions that may take months & years to work out in a few hours. I wish I knew if this bores you. I'm afraid it does. And all is of no consequence because it's just drivel that I say & write at times. Heaven knows if I believe them or not. It seems ages since I heard from you. I expect work is keeping you busy. What do you think of it?

[*Dorothy began working on 11 May*]

Now I'm in two minds if I'll send this or not. I'll have to get it in an envelope & stamped & addressed quick. I never know & have never known what exactly to write you girl. I mean that anything I have to say seems quite silly & a waste of time to say it when I read over a letter. And I'm afraid I don't really know what you do think of things. That is I believe you think you see! I wouldn't find it any effort to stop you know. In fact it might be a relief. I wonder if you can see I am trying to show you some things that interest me, And I can never know somehow if you are interested in them or just listening – you see I will often listen to people though I think they are talking piffle or though I know them to be wrong, just to study the idea & how it is got. Well I don't want you to study ideas from me. Because I wouldn't say anything on a serious subject unless I thought the other person was interested. Simply because I'm shy I suppose in these things. I guess you won't understand Dorothy. Never mind. There isn't much worth worrying about in this old world. Just one or two things which I am sure you would disagree with me on. Chiefly because you have been taught one way & and I have found another. Nevertheless yours may be quite right & more worthy. Oh I don't know – there are so many ways of getting to a place. But I chiefly believe your own system of just living in the present & the future sort of crazy. Sometimes I think it's weak but when I consider the results of looking ahead, I realise it's the only thing. So you laugh because you must even it it is a joke or not. Poor girl! Well I won't inflict more. But some of this I would have said only how could I with your eyes laughing at me? And much better & possibly more important things to do!

John S. Riggs

11 May, 1917

Dear Girl,

I was expecting your letter soon. I haven't had your one written on the 2nd worse luck. I did have one from your mother postmarked 3rd, but none from you. What have you done with it? I thought maybe your labours had exhausted you & so was not cross!

As you know quite well Miss I did not intend to insult your intelligence when I didn't send the book. Just it struck me differently afterwards. If you understand you do, if not I'm afraid I can't explain any fuller. Really I know you just say these things to tease.

Our work is still the same. When we have gun drill or other strenuous games in the sun we usually sleep through the afternoon's lecture. Air around here does make you sleepy & fat. Yes, I know we wouldn't get much exchange if I didn't talk seriously sometimes, but exchange was just what worried me. Because you so seldom are serious (not that I want you to be girl) that I was afraid I was inflicting views on you that couldn't interest you. I suppose you are serious sometimes aren't you?

Do you realise (maybe I shouldn't tell you this, give you ideas above yourself!) that you get almost as much per week as I do? I am supposed to earn 21/- a week. Of course I don't. But my real value to the army is much more than that. When they see this I will start & earn it! And yet after all your sermons about waste in war-time she goes and buys silk stockings. Not that I think you shouldn't but you cannot claim that silk is necessary. If you just want to swank sure silk feet would be enough as the rest doesn't show! The Hat of course is useful. One of the floppy kind that hangs over your features. You would then protect yourself from attentions caused by so much beauty shown at once!

I thought you liked the manager when you went to be interviewed. I'm sorry you haven't a nicer place to work in. At least in some ways I'm glad because you don't really realise the value of things till you go without. And yet I hate the idea of you having to do these things. You may not understand why you more than anyone else. Well I don't & wouldn't have any girl I know working in those conditions. It's just selfishness really. I won't tell you what I think of you for doing it. I don't quite know why you do it though, at least I do in a way, but it seems a strange reason to me. It's not to please yourself & I'm such a selfish person that unless things please me I wouldn't do them. Oh, all nonsense! Wash out in signals W.W.

I haven't had any buzzer test yet. We have had a lot of tests in the last week here – they aren't exams. You must pass the exams, but you may not in which case you try again. See? Are you still going to be a perfect lady when you have worked. A "perfect lady" didn't do anything so common as work? Yes, infant I am interested. And you know it really or you wouldn't write it. And I'm not shy that way. It's just I realise what small margins carry most people's interests. Mine aren't wide I know & you always have a tendency to judge others by yourself. Anyway if in future you are bored you have only yourself to blame.

I am certain that neither your breakfast or dinner is a light matter, but I'm honoured that you postpone such important things for me. Honestly girl I don't believe you realise how grateful I really am. I can't tell you how much your letters do mean. Of course to prevent you being too proud – I have nothing else in the way of pleasures here! And every little pleasure is better than none!

I am pleased to hear about your hair – will it really stand out this time – I wish there wasn't so long till I could try. [*Dorothy had beautiful long auburn hair shown tied under a scarf in a picture of her in 'munitions' uniform.*]

John S. Riggs

12 May, 1917

Dearest Girl,

Why I'm writing this I don't know. I haven't really anything to say & it's just an excuse for the postman to call on you. <u>Anything</u> is welcome from the post isn't it, at least I have always found it so. Chiefly because we are in spite of all our arguments still children & young. So when you don't know what I <u>was</u> going to say – honest Dorothy – my pen just ran away. Do you know the clear-est memory I have of you is, well the two clearest. One in the car the last day (when it rained) & the other that Sunday we played in the kitchen when you came down from the other end of the table & laughed. Awfully silly isn't it girl. Perfectly ridiculous pleasure!

Your letter hasn't as yet turned up. I'm sorry because your mother said you would tell me about all the humour in the works. Supper having turned up I must stop – even more important than you!

John S. Riggs

Dorothy with the Triumph, 15 June, 1917

13 May, 1917

Dear Mrs Kendall,

This is just a note. Why I don't quite know. I've been writing letters all afternoon & thought I would add another before I toddle to bed. I've discovered what has been worrying me for the last while. I'm afraid I gave way to it & told you. Which I shouldn't have & I'm sorry. You must think it rotten of me to be always on the grouse. Well it was this. That I hated to see the men enjoying themselves the way most do. In which wine, women & song play a large part. You'll think me an awful prig but I dislike it. And I didn't like to see these men who could be so splendid like that. I know that they can't be judged on that. You'll think what awful rot and I won't say it but to you. Forget it & the grouses now. I only say it to explain the grouses & it's quite all right now.

John S. Riggs

16 May, 1917

Dear Dorothy,

You don't deserve this you know. Being treated far too well. Anyway it's only a note because I hoped to get a letter today & it hasn't come. Munitions are a terrible thing.

I have no excuse for writing. Except that it pleases you to see the postman and I was going to enclose a letter from France from Sgt Panting. I wasn't though because you mightn't like it even though you did want to get letters from France. Maybe other people's letters wouldn't satisfy the "curio" taste. I'll really not worry you again till I hear. I hear a rumour of the Irish boats being held up but of course don't know it it's true or not.

I'm feeling fearfully sleepy but I have still a little work to do. I think you had better be left alone for a while.

John S. Riggs

16 May, 1917

Dear Dorothy,

I _am_ sorry. I crawl! After I had posted my letter I went over to dinner & lo & behold there was your letter – the post it seems was very late today. I expect this will reach you the same time as the last one. I can't stop to write now, but your letter <u>was</u> liked. And the sketches are much admired. You _are_ a nice girl sometimes (last added to prevent conceit). I'm glad you do buy things because they are nice. I may laugh at her but really (and she knows it) I love her to look nice. Why? Don't ask me questions.

I don't know if I'll get time to write you tomorrow, because we have an exam on Friday & I will require a towel & plenty of cold water. It's on Military Law & King's Regulations. Subject which I hate. There is no justice in the Army & discipline I don't believe in the way they do. Anyway girl what you said about my letters being looked for went right home because I have been that way so often myself. Getting back dead-tired & hoping against hope that there will be a letter. From anyone if not the best. So I'll try & write soon. So good-night girl dear.

John S. Riggs

18 May, 1917

Dear Dorothy,

I'm afraid I didn't write last night. I was rather pushed for time & I had to do a little work for the Exam. I think by the way that the result will be all right unless they knock off marks for bad writing & spelling. The information was all there anyway. Do you remember Captain Kettle's engineer in one of the yarns called "The Frying Pan" who couldn't get a chief's ticket because the Board of Trade inspectors didn't like his spelling?

I doubt if this will reach you before Monday unless you have a Sunday delivery. Rather a pity because I might write again in the week-end & then you would get them together. And I know that isn't good for you & doesn't mean so much as on separate days.

I haven't yet seen any sign of wings or a halo but perhaps in time – I don't <u>think</u> angels ever grin you know. Please go on being silly!

I didn't think you were grousing when you wrote but I can see lots of things you don't mention and it seems different from Gertie's place. Who told you I didn't object to Gertie working? I felt much the same only didn't dare say so to anyone. I talked to Gertie though & she told me they were chiefly in fact all her own sort. It's not the work I object to. Sure you know that. It's the people.* Though if you judge aright they are most good somewhere – sometimes I admit hard to see. And if you remember I thought you should though I didn't like the idea. I think Nina should though I would rather she didn't. Like you want to remain young always, but realise you must do your share in the world's work which means you have to leave a certain youth behind (though in thought you may be always young). See? Girl. I am certain you will gain more than you lose anyway when you recognise your part. I do hope you won't adopt any of your fellow workers' methods of face decoration. Soap & water is much better. Besides <u>I</u> should have to be awful careful of it when I see you! It might get patchy and that <u>would</u> be worse than hair wouldn't it? I'm so pleased your stockings are nice! I hope they won't be worn out before I get home. You <u>will</u> have a lot of swagger clothes to be admired in.

And please I'm not "respectable" – I have visions when that word is used of black tall shiny hats & umbrellas neatly rolled. Church twice a day & take round the plate. I can't see to write more. I'm writing by the window & it has got too dark <u>and</u> it's nearly bed time. Good night girl.

John S. Riggs

[*Presumably he is referring to a social division between privately educated, middle-class girls who volunteered to work, and the working-class girls who had no choice but to work in the foundry.]

28 May, 1917

Dear Girl,

I'm sorry I'm longer than usual in answering. We are having a very "windy" time & keep discovering things we know nothing about. Didn't even know they existed. So I spend time which might otherwise be spent in writing you in trying to learn a little.

Your letter was awfully welcome & the photo is quite beyond me to thank you for. Really it's quite like you except that you look much too good. How did you manage to hold that expression for long enough! Really I like it. Nuff said! I honestly admit your tongue or pen rather is too much for me. It is the cheekiness that leaves me gasping & wondering what you'll really be like when you grow up. Sorry you are grown up. I forgot for a minute!

The exam papers we've had so far were elementary so I couldn't be brilliant. It's the next and last exam that really counts & which does take some passing I think. Oh, and you may remember the yarn about the course being lengthened. Well it has been to four months now. We won't have it all, and may escape having any. Doubtful yet. The last joined squads will do the full four months.

No, I didn't think it was likely you would try & cover your beauty with paint. Because you're too proud of it. Honestly girl you know I wasn't serious. And it isn't a pity your hair isn't the same colour. I prefer it as it is thank you. Doubtless you have your own idea but please I'm quite content. Yes, you did call me a "respectable" old soldier. But you weren't serious so what matter. I only mentioned it as a false classification for me. You'll find this a very silly letter I guess. Really I am just rambling on so that I can say you have had a letter and that there is one due to me. Always you know after a letter I feel slightly disappointed. Not in your letters girl. Not that. But when you're expecting a letter you have it to look forward to every post time & when you've just got one you know there isn't much chance of there being one for you. See what I mean. I sometimes carry your letters round for a day (if I get them in the morning) just to gloat over the fact that you <u>have</u> a letter which you haven't read yet. Sounds mad doesn't it. I haven't much longer to spend on this. Must rush off and dress for dinner. I suppose you are going on working all summer or when do you have a holiday? And where would you be going if you were. I should be home next month, but it might be later. You haven't bought any more clothes have you? Let them be real swank when you do. Help to make up for your other failings. No, girl, you're just you & that's the beginning & end.

Good night Dorothy, John S. Riggs

I'm dissatisfied with this letter someway, but I'll send it. Be merciful.

30 May, 1917

Dear Girl,

Your letter came yesterday evening. Really if you carry on teaching me French at the rate you do I'll be able to speak it well when I go across again. And that will be nice. Before we just talked English and a weird mixture of Flemish & French. Could always or nearly always get understood. My dear cheild! When did I ever pretend to know everything – I always admitted how hopelessly inferior in knowledge I was to a certain young lady. Oh by the way the Sen. Q? [*illeg.*] here called us gentlemen today! Must be <u>some</u> truth in it.

I didn't say definitely that I passed the last exam all right. I've passed all the practical exams or tests rather, except telephones which I'm not frightened of and a field day combined thing that we do tomorrow. The final exam is the written one on Monday.

I hope you won't be on overtime when I get back, because I would see so terribly little of you. Could you dare take a day or so off? You wouldn't be slacking really when you have been so hard at it all the rest of the time. I think your mother would agree. Anyway I could put up with your crossness I think. I can be very patient. And I know you wouldn't be cross for long. Dorothy dear I didn't want to be sarcastic about you and I wasn't trying to rub anything in. Please forgive me & I'll crawl again as you said you liked it. Only it's <u>very</u> undignified!

No girl you were not "fishing". I <u>know</u> you better than you think, I believe, and its not what you would do unless in fun. Still I may have my own opinions of your appearance may I not?

I have seen nearly all the Ulster Players pieces – except any within the last three years. The two you mentioned I thought among the best. Thompson for the reason you mentioned as well as for its own. I'm tempted to repeat the expression I'm forbidden to use. Only I can understand quite well. It is the one thing will often make me do things if I'm told I can't. A 6 inch filled weight is about 100 lbs – do you know if that's the weight of yours filled? [*Presumably this refers to the shell cases Dorothy was making.*] Despite your many lectures on obedience I <u>think</u> you could do with some yourself. I'll have to see about it!

There's not a lot to tell you. Our squad ("K") has got itself a name for being smart. Awful lie really, but a good bluff. Very few married men or old men with us as some of the other squads have. We have also to our misfortune been the cause of one or two rows after lights out & been jumped on as a result. Still we bear up! I'll try to squeeze in another letter in a few days. Did I tell you there is a daughter in this house who's very shy. We've hardly seen her but last night she appeared to bring us supper. We were overcome. Purser the Naval Division man has spent many hours trying to scrape aquaintance with her and failed so far. Now when his time is nearly up she appears. He's going to be married too as soon as he leaves here! Such are men – untrustworthy creatures!

Getting late. We're starting early tomorrow so I must toddle off to bed. There isn't the temptation to stay up till 11 p.m. or so here, and there's no one to say goodnight to at the porch! Goodnight girl dear.

John S. Riggs

4 June, 1917

Dear Girl,

I had your letter some five hours ago and I'm answering it at once. I'm glad that you are leaving the other place – isn't it Mackie's Gertie is at? You wouldn't have such long hours there would you? I got your PC on Saturday. Your imprudence takes my breath away and leaves me so that I can only smile feebly. Have you <u>no</u> respect for your elders and betters?!

The daughter of this house doesn't interest me. And my influence with the gentlemen is nil. We don't have much in common though we live together quite happy. That is one thing the old army does teach you, you silly kid! I'm jolly pleased (though I shouldn't tell you this really) you had the temper to go anyway. Your comment "it was worth it" is the spirit. You'll do Dorothy – but children shouldn't be encouraged to be naughty you know! Still you're getting a big girl now and able to judge, as I used to be told, "the real value of money" but I don't think that's a decent thing to keep drumming into a kid.

We had our final exam today. I think I may have just squeezed through. I'll know the result on some time on Wednesday. If I am through I'll leave here on Friday and hope to see you Saturday. If I don't pass I'll write and tell you. Anyway you can guess I'll come to see you just as soon as I get back no matter when it is. Been fearfully hot today – not ideal for exams. There isn't much to do now except wait.

John S. Riggs

Dorothy's diary:

Sunday 9 June: <u>A Year Ago</u> – Jack came home from Trowbridge. I was at the Bank in the morning, but he came about 3.30 & we talked for a long time in the garden. Chess, talk etc. in the evening. He stayed till about 10.45.

Monday 10: <u>A Year Ago</u> – sat in the garden all morning. Jack and Gertie came up about 4.30 to ask me to go for a walk. We didn't go till after tea, then we took the tram to the terminal and walked over Queen's grounds to the bluebell wood. Home again a little after 9. Gertie went on into town & Jack came home with me for supper.

Tuesday 11: <u>A Year Ago</u> – my first time at Mackies 3 – 9. Jack was at Lurgan all day.

Wednesday 12: <u>A Year Ago</u> – Jack came about 11 & we went for a walk over Queen's grounds. Took a lot of photos etc. Back about 1 – Jack stayed to dinner [*lunch?*]. Mackies from 3 – 9.

Thursday 13: <u>A Year Ago</u> – Nothing much in the morning – Mackies 3 – 9. Jack and Gertie came round about 5. I saw them again when I was going to tea at 5.30.

Friday 14: <u>A Year Ago</u> – Jack arrived with a Triumph motor bike & sidecar about 10.30. We went for paraffin & then went up Stockman's Lane towards Colin. I learned to drive it. Mackies 3 – 9. Jack & Gertie came to take me home.

Saturday 15: <u>A Year Ago</u> – Jack came about 10.30 with Nina and the kid Muriel in the sidecar – Nina & kid went home almost immediately & Jack & I went out for a run. Round by Ballyaughlis & up a by-road to Drumbo. Got a puncture on the way home just before B'aughlis. Made us rather late in getting home – Mackies 3 – 9. Jack was there when I got home as he had been to tea with Mother. Took her out in the sidecar round by Osborne Park. Then took Daddy the same way.

Jack with his new Triumph, 16 June, 1917

Sunday 16: <u>A Year Ago</u> – Jack came up and took me out. First we called at Chambers in Donegall Place, then we went through town to the Bond to get my last week's pay. Out to Knock & back. I bought some khaki hankies at A & McAuley's while Jack went to his tailors to get my badge. Then to G.P.O. to cash my pay – then to Easons to get him a book I wanted him to read. Called at the Bank to leave some things in. Then home. Mackies. Jack brought me home in sidecar – stayed to supper.

Monday 17: <u>A Year Ago</u> – Jack & Nina came for sidecar about 10.30 went out in it. Sat in the garden till about 4.30. Walk after tea – up Newforge & back from mill dam across fields by Somersets new house – neither of them stayed to supper.

Tuesday 18: <u>A Year Ago</u> – Jack came about 3.45 & stayed for tea & supper – can't remember what we did – chess amongst other things.

Wednesday 19: <u>A Year Ago</u> – Mackies 9 – 1.30 got out early. Jack came & did photos in the afternoon. In the evening we went & met Nina & went up the river. Jack came back to supper here.

Thursday 20: <u>A Year Ago</u> – Jack met me in Donegall Place after I came from Mackies and came up with me. Photographs all afternoon – went up the river in the evening – didn't go through the slip. Did a bit of exploring in Belvoir Park – started to rain as we were coming home. Jack stayed to supper.

Friday 21: <u>A Year Ago</u> – Jack came up in the afternoon & developed and printed photos till about 10.45. I went to bed before he left.

Saturday 22: <u>A Year Ago</u> – Mackies 9 to 3. Jack came early in the afternoon & went about 8 as Nina had told him she had some people coming in. It was a false alarm however. Printing, enlarging etc. all afternoon.

Sunday 23: <u>A Year Ago</u> – Mackies 9 to 3, arranged for Jack to come round on Monday with Mother. He came up in the afternoon & did photos all evening. Very showery.

Monday 24: <u>A Year Ago</u> – Sat in the garden practically all day. Jack didn't arrive till tea time as he had been with Gertie at Helen Stewarts. Daddy took some photos after tea. Jack was very riotous!

Tuesday 25: <u>A Year Ago</u> – Jack came up in the morning & did photos. Stayed to dinner. Mother came round Mackies about 4 o'clock.

Wednesday 26: <u>A Year Ago</u> – Jack brought shoes & we went out for a walk up by Shaw's Bridge & back along the towing path & Newforge. John S. very grumpy. Mackies 3 to 9. Jack met me at corner of Springfield & Great Victoria Street & came part of the way up with me.

Thursday 27: A Year Ago – Jack came up to go for a walk just as I was ready to go down town, however I changed and went with him. Over the old golf course by sand pits – home about 1. Mackies 3 till 9.

Friday 28: A Year Ago – Jack looked in for about half an hour in the morning. I went shopping. Mackies 3 to 9.

Saturday 29: A Year Ago – Jack was here all morning doing photos & enlargements. He came up to tea with Mother too and was here when I came back from Mackies at 9.30. Stayed to supper.

Sunday 30: A Year Ago – Jack came for me and we went up the river – landed in Belvoir grounds and explored a bit – home about 1 in time for me to get ready for Mackies.

Monday 1: A Year Ago – Very fine day, sat in the garden. Daddy took some photos. I went down to the Bank for tea. John S. very grumpy, but cheered up a bit after tea when explaining the innards of the old motorbike. Mr Laurie was there. Jack came home with me and stayed to supper.

Puncture, 15 June, 1917

Dorothy and her father at 47 Adelaide Park

Tuesday 2: <u>A Year Ago</u> – Mackies 9 till 3. Jack was here in the afternoon and evening.

Wednesday 3: <u>A Year Ago</u> – Mackies 9 till 3. Jack came in the afternoon & stayed for tea and until about 8.30. Daddy and I went down to the boat with him as all the Bank people had gone to Portrush. We took a good many photos in the evening.

> *R.A. Mess, Cooden Camp,*
> *Bexhill, Sussex 12 July, 1917*

Dear Girl,

I'm sorry (I seem to be always saying that to you) but I thought you would guess why I didn't write – you did partly it seems. This can only be a note as I'm writing between parades and have only a few minutes. I'll write fuller tonight. But I <u>did</u> mean to write after a week and it was only when I started to last night that I remembered I hadn't your holiday address. You will doubtless be interested to hear we are better fed than I've ever been in my life. Result is I'm getting fatter than ever. Really if "overseas" doesn't come soon I'll be like the late lamented John Bunny? of picture fame. I haven't time to say anything serious just now. Yes, I can hear the sigh of relief! But I'll try to explain tonight – cheerio.

> John S. Riggs

R. A. Mess, Cooden Camp,
Bexhill, Sussex

12 July, 1917

Dear Girl,

I'm writing this after dinner, and having that tired feeling. This isn't all due to dinner, but we took a boat out and had a most enjoyable swim from it. First time I've been in sea water since the outbreak of war I believe. Last time was when we were camping in the Mournes.

Well about why I didn't write. As you guessed I had & still have the idea that it was better not. You see I thought if I just tried to forget for a week or so I could then promise I think to treat you properly as a chum. And I <u>know</u> you would rather have that. I can now if you'll help. Only please girl don't try and tease me into breaking away when you don't want it really. You see I rather let myself go since I came back and knew you. You maybe don't quite understand but I wasn't quite so "case hardened" if I can put it that way as I usually am. I told you things and did things with you that I would despise myself for being so damned weak if it was anyone else. And again I'm nearly sure, or was, that you were just sorry because I was someone to fool with & even <u>I</u> don't <u>like</u> my friends leaving anywhere when I know they don't want to go.

You see when I found that you <u>knew</u> you didn't really know, it gave me such a chance of sneering at myself. Sometimes I thought well anyway sometime she will care if I get back. Yes, and then I thought it worthwhile trying to come back on that chance? And some devil of madness in me says no. So I just care even more and think of some mad things to do. I'm afraid this must seem rather contradictory in places but I jerk up and down a lot. Sometimes it's the best of worlds and worth living & other times well it's hell. You see war has this effect on me and on most men. It makes men and beasts. Well I vary. Sometimes I'm an awful beast and other times quite happy to be a man & live & suffer with men. Just to be a strong beast and force things your way. You know I'm sure this isn't good for you at all. I'm giving myself away horribly & to a girl who only laughs. All right laugh miss. <u>I'll</u> try not to show anything till I can hit back and then I will laugh. Rather a cruel laugh because I'll remember what I've put up with.

Still if you'll help and let the past go we'll just be chums, if you want it so. I'm afraid though I want such a lot from my friends that you won't like it. I am prepared to give myself in return but there aren't many who want anything to do with me. In France things were different. People would do things for you – God only knows why. But you could trust them & you did. I wonder could you understand the way in which you know that someone would take the finest risks just for you and to be able to count on it. Well enough of this you don't really know anything yet cheild! When you grow up!

No, I wasn't offended because you didn't weep. I didn't expect you to. You're much too full of respect for appearances for one thing and too young to understand sorrow except as a child would for a lost toy. Poor Dorothy. It's not fair to expect her to grow up.

You know when I found I hadn't your Donegal address I was quite resolved to waiting till you came back. I admit it would have been beastly & I should have washed it off on some mad jaunt or other. You can you know when you're unhappy forget it all by taking risks so that you haven't time to think. This is rather a serious letter for you. I <u>won't</u> crawl though because some day you may remember & be wise. Wise men get wisdom from fools or words to that effect – I forget just how it goes.

Well they tell us when we finish here that our lot at present are booked for home batteries. That is batteries in training you know. Conscripts most of 'em. Which I don't think I'd like. And England when there's no one to love you is rather slow. So I shan't be sorry if they have to send us as reinforcements. Not that I'm any more satisfied with artillery, but I'd like to see a little of the work in France with them before I decide to change, and there isn't much time to do all I want to do. It's getting so dark I can't see, and they shut the club house at 10.30. I must up to camp where things are on the move nearly all night. I was approached by one man here today who knew me at school. We had quite an interesting talk as it was about 1912 when I saw him last.

Good night girl, and please don't be cross longer than you can help.

John S. Riggs

R.A. Mess, Cooden Camp,
18 July, 1917

Dear Girl,

I shouldn't really be writing again But I can't help it. Besides you like to get <u>anything</u> by post (even a bill?) so maybe you'll put up with this because it has a stamp on it. I think now it must have appeared an extremely foolish letter I wrote yesterday. But I can't help saying the most foolish things to you often things I don't mean, and sometimes things are all mixed. No wonder the poor girl is frightened sometimes. You know I feel awfully ashamed of myself for the way I spoilt you. I don't mean pulling your ears (I'm sorry for that too though you <u>did</u> deserve it!) Nor do I mean that you got your own way or anything, but just you aren't quite the same. And I should have known better even if you didn't. You couldn't be expected to whereas I could. You know girl dear you'll have to try & control me a little because I can't myself.

It was most awfully decent of you to write to me before you went away. I didn't think you would care enough too [*sic*]. Fact I didn't think you would be hurt if I didn't write. I don't want to hurt <u>you</u> girl. I thought you might be relieved than otherwise because when I said it would take so long to reach you with a letter you only giggled (as usual). And I find it hard sometimes to undersand anything from a giggle. You didn't really say you'd write at once so I took it you weren't anxious. You must admit girl you don't tell me much and I'm afraid I'm a stupid person in believing things. Still I won't forget that you

<u>did</u> write. Very dear of you really. I don't expect I'll have a chance to write in the week-end as we hope (my half section & I) to go to Hastings.

Oh, Dorothy when we went down to bathe this evening a "Girls School" was in! So they haven't all left this part of the coast. I think it's a big building just behind our camp. I'm afraid they are too well looked after though. Have to see what Hastings can produce. You know I don't think you made a great success of my training. Do you admit failure or have just given up, or do you still hope? It's getting dark again – must toddle. There seems quite a chance that we'll go straight from here without leave. Horrid! But if it was France it wouldn't be so bad. <u>Must</u> stop. Good night girl.

John S. Riggs

Cooden Camp, Bexhill
21 July, 1917

Dear Girl,

I could of course have written sooner but I didn't. I think this will just reach you when you get back. It should anyway. I'm just lazing through the afernoon waiting for tea, with your letter for company. No one else here though it's a fine place & commands a wide view. Beachy Head on one side & all the beach right along to Cooden. There is the golf links just below where various lunatics are chasing white balls about. Just think if I live long enough I may come to that as a <u>sport</u>!

I'm afraid I can't believe all you say in your letter. It was dear of you to write it but well but – I have my own opinion. To start with you have a lot of time to yourself & not a great deal to keep so busy so you would feel things more. I hate people to do things that way. I'd far rather have the trust and be hurt, at least the old gods don't get much of a laugh then. Well I would have warned you I wouldn't write if I'd thought you would mind. Only well I didn't. I'm glad you are having such a good time. Must be a jolly place. How do you keep out of mischief? [*Gweedore Hotel, Co. Donegal*]

At present I loaf round the camp & appear clever. Oh yes, I can look that way when its wanted. Only usually a blank dull look pays ever so much more. Because they think "Oh he's thick" & he doesn't get too much to do. You want to know your man though before you try it – dull look is best on the average.

Oh, many thanks for the photos. It <u>was</u> an oversight. I don't know where I've put them now but they are somewhere around. Do you <u>really dress</u> for dinner? How wonderful! And remember to say "thank you not any more" when you are asked. Leastways those were the manners for little girls in my young days.

About a Home battery. I don't know quite how long because it depends at what stage you join the battery. Only not more than another 6 months. I think it will be overseas for most of us. Demand is heavy just now & work is supposed to be practical artillery only it isn't. It's the usual way you train at home – for France nothing practical. Leastways its not the way you do it in France.

I expect to get an extra shilling a day when I pass this exam. So far I haven't done anything & don't intend to. I don't care if I pass or not so I'm out every evening in Hastings or Bexhill.

I expect tomorrow – Sunday – I'll go up to Battle for the day. Its where the Battle of Hastings was fought & is worth seeing I believe. Anyway I'll see it if only because it was the only date besides 55 BC. I ever knew. And yet I used to get high marks in History till I stopped work. My last year at Inst was a glorious rag. I knew then at least I had decided I was going into the shops and would have to work up again so I didn't care. It was worth it – sure.

There is a chance then, particularly if we are for overseas, that I get over to Ireland before the end of the week. Even if I only get a few days I'll come because No! I shan't say it! Then you'll be conceited. But honestly I don't know quite what you want me to be. I'm quite prepared to be anything even if I don't know how! Can find out I suppose? It's nearly tea time & I want to get into slacks before I wander out. I think I'll make it Hastings this evening. And there will be a tram back seeing its Saturday: on week nights last tram's about 8 p. m. & we only reach there about 7 or so. So we come back by train to Bexhill & then taxi when we can find one. Last night we arrived about 11.30 with some dozen or so in the taxi. Some squeeze! I'm still in hopes of finding someone to love me. Nobody round the golf house – and there are plenty of girls – seems to. Horrid of them I call it. But I'm very glad they don't. There isn't any sense in this letter any way. Nor any real nonsense. It's just scribble all the way. But then that's best. I wonder when you are really going to get sense.

We had quite a happy day on Thursday tramping across country on a field day stunt. Awful foolish but it pleases the army to play at soldiers. Really. Dear girl I'm afraid you'll get bullied again unless you exercise a strong influeance. But I'll try not to. Only you'll have to help. I really must toddle but I would like you here for once. You are a bad *enfant* you know & want spanking really. I think your father didn't give you half enough.

Well really yours, John S. Riggs

Engagement

Dorothy's diary for July/August 1918 written at Greencastle, Co. Donegal

Sunday 28: Church at 12. Bathed after lunch – Yanks arrived just after tea, played with them till dinner time & after – great fun.
A Year Ago – Jack came home and was up here about 10.30. Stayed to dinner & went as far as the pass with me to try & get a bus of some sort. Mackies 3 to 9. When I got home he had got a BSA, but had the magneto all to bits as it wouldn't go. Left about 10.45.

Monday 29: Short walk along sands – bathed – after lunch lounged. After tea fishing & tennis. Strolled around after dinner.
A Year Ago – Jack was here practically all day & put the bike together. Rained most of the day – got bus going just before tea & went out on it. I drove most of the way to Lurgan & back. Called on the Menarys – Jack stayed to supper.

Tuesday 30: Letter from Mother [*Dorothy must have been staying as a guest of the family at Drumaweir Hotel which was owned by her friend Gertie's parents.*] Bathed and played croquet after tea. After dinner went for a little walk – just back when the American Navy men came. Went out in the car with them – lovely drive – nearly to Malin.
A Year Ago – Mackies 9 till 2. Came home with something in my eye. Jack came about 4 & we sat in the garden till tea, then out in the sidecar round by Ballyaughlis, Drumbo & Lisburn – home by hill road.

Wednesday 31: Sat about all morning till bathing time. Loafed after lunch. In the evening went out & met the American Navy who were coming down. Took the car down to the Hermitage and got Let Colhoun to come back. Two cars full were here. Danced till about mid-night – sing song afterwards.
A Year Ago – Mackies 9 to 3. Jack brought me home. We went for a joy ride up by Colin Glen & back along the hill through Crumlin & Ligoniel. Home about 6 o'clock.

Thursday 1: Sat about or practised till bathing time. After lunch sat about till tea. After dinner went for a wee walk then played patience till about 10. Three Yanks arrived then & we danced till 11.45.
A Year Ago – Mackies 9 – 3. Jack brought me home – sat in the garden in the afternoon. Went to Ballynahinch & home by Hillsborough in the bus in the evening.

Friday 2: Walked into Moville in the morning & got Jimmie's present. Bathed after lunch, then croquet till dinner time. Two loads of Yanks from Jura arrived – dancing in the boat-house till 11.30 or so. Great time.
A Year Ago – Stayed at home all morning with my knee. Jack called in for bus – went to Downpatrick in the bus in the evening – home about 6.30. Jim Easthope was there all evening.

Saturday 3: Lounged till bathing time. Very fine day. Lounged and drew pictures of all our Navy visitors. Doc. & Mrs Gory arrived about 5.30 and we bathed again. Dinner at the Hermitage with them – back to dance here 9 – 11.30. Gorgeous time.
A Year Ago – Stayed at home again. Jack called for bus as usual. In the afternoon went to see the doc. about my knee – was laid up for a fortnight – not to walk or anything. Jack got me chocs and stayed till about 8.30 – then had to go as Nina expected some friends.

Sunday 4: Very wet morning – practised till I o'clock then went for a wee walk with Alboid[?] Up to cross-roads & back. Two more car loads arrived in the afternoon. Nice family tea party. Croquet till bathing time – walk in the garden. Short row with Lenlon, Ostrich, Bass & Doc.
A Year Ago – Stuck in garden all day lounging. Jack there most of the time.

Monday 5: Walk to Greencastle in the morning – climbed all climbable places. Rained all afternoon. Went & sketched Jimmie. Cards & music in the evening.
A Year Ago – Sat in the garden all day. Daddy, Mother & family went out on bus in the evening.

Tuesday 6: Short walk along sands & back. Bathed in beastly low tide – all weedy & horrible. Picnic with Gertie along sands for tea. McIvor brought Mr McBride & Mr Stevenson back fairly late, having lost a wheel on the way. Walking, talking & music till about 11.30.
A Year Ago – Jack was up in the afternoon & evening. We got engaged about 8.30.

Wednesday 7: Bathed in the morning. Ostrich & Jabriski came down for golf. Doc & Gorey arrived by the post motor about 4.45. They bathed & then went to dinner at the Hermitage. Dancing till 11.30. Great fun. Mr Gilliland had a stroke.

<u>A Year Ago</u> – Jack brought Nina up in the morning & then took me down to buy the ring. He was up all afternoon & till about 8 in the evening. *

Thursday 8: Very unsettled & stormy day. Doc & Lenlon arrived on the Indian about 9.30 & left about 10.45.

*This is the last entry relating to John S's home leave. There is no reference to his departure, presumably the next day. After Jack's death Dorothy threw the opal ring into the sea at Orlock, Co. Down.

> *Cranston's Waverley Hotel,*
> *Southampton Row, London WC1*
> *12 p.m. 8 August, 1917*

Dear Girl,

Just look at the time I'm writing this so don't expect much. I'll try & write again tomorrow before I leave. I got down to Bexhill in time to get my warrant and orders to leave London by 11.35 a.m. tomorrow for Southampton which means *La Belle France.* I expect we may be at the base there a few days or maybe only hours. Anyway I can't give you an address till I arrive. I'm sorry. Just think of me waiting all that time for a letter!

Say Girl did you ever read *The Valley of the Moon* by Jack London, if you haven't you might because it says a lot that I would like you to read. Perfectly mad of course. Been a good Girl since? I suppose so simply from lack of chance to be anything else! You don't lack will I'm sure. You know girl I wish I hadn't been so rough with you at times. You must exercise will & slap me or something. And I'm afraid I was horrid when we were down town on Tuesday. I am sorry kid but I didn't mean to be, only I felt so little use in the operation and I did want you to be satisfied.

Good night Dorothy chum,

> John S. Riggs

> *R.G.A. Base, B.E.F.*
> *11 August, 1917*

Dear Dorothy,

You'll note address. I expect I'll be leaving here in a day or two as we are under orders now, but anyway they will forward and I expect before you write again that I'll be able to send my next address.

We crossed from Southampton that night. Quite a nice crossing & so much better than my previous ones as the boat wasn't crowded. We toddled round the place here in the morning (anyone can tell you where one usually goes from Southampton) and separated at the depot here in the afternoon. Since then just loafed and slept. We did a gas course this mornng or I would have written then.

There isn't anything else material to write and somehow I can't express things just now. You'll be interested to hear my friend James Henderson got engaged not married while on leave. I'm afraid you'll think I'm an awful unfeeling brute but I'm not really. Only I got so used to being hardened when I came away from home and not looking forward to anything that it seems unbelievable that I have now. And I'm certain you don't know the happiness there is in having something to hope for. It's great. You know when I got back to France from my last leave I honestly didn't care if I went again. Now I am quite content to hope for a leave as soon as possible knowing you'll be there. Perfectly daft isn't it kid. But – oh – you know how I feel I'd like to tear this up because it doesn't say anything I want to say. I'll leave just now and finish later. It's raining like the devil just now. John.

Later – Somehow I can't really write you tonight, so you'll just have to count this a note. I should hear in a week if you write shortly after you get this.

I should have told you that most of my Trowbridge Squad are here as they sent two classes from Bexhill. Makes it quite jolly.

You remember the afternoon we went to Ballynahinch? Somehow it sticks clearer because somehow we understood better. And it was I think the last time you drove wasn't it. You know it gave me a very real pleasure to have you driving. And doing it well (<u>Don't</u> get . . .) I hadn't much confidence myself in <u>driving</u>, of course there <u>were</u> other things). I'm sorry *enfant* there doesn't seem more to say. I can't write just now. And yet I want to. Only it seems silly to try & put things on paper. Understand? I'll get used to it & then I will be able to. Meanwhile I'll wait contentedly till I hear from you.

Yours, John S. Riggs

Gaul, 13 August, 1917

My dear Dorothy,

It is my turn to begin by a Christian name! Thanks ever so much for the parcel – everyone liked it so much that I hardly got anything but the mittens! What is your grievance against those useful garments? I have no pretensions to being a connoisseur of such things, cut they seem to be just my size and shape, & they are certainly thick & warm. As you prefer a censored letter to a green envelope, I will try to push this past the eagle eye of the authorities.

ANSWERS TO CORRESPONDENTS

I. My address was the "Distillery" in very truth, for we were then living in an attic over a distillery We are now in a . . . More anon. Anyway, I kept sober <u>most</u> of the time!

II. In your reply you should refer to the mystic number because, when I turn up my Correspondence ledger, I find an entry to the effect that No. 606 was to you on such a date containing so & so. Some sort of system is absolutely necessary, as I write such vast numbers of letters. (In reply to this, please mention No. 1772).

III. As regards my life being full of danger – you can hardly imagine the manifold risks I run daily. Perhaps a short description of a typical run may be of interest – leaving the comparative safety of a shell-devastated office, I dash down a winding road full of bucking mules & skidding motors, & pitted here & there with shell holes the size of a small mustard mine; the bullets whiz-z-z by me, & shrapnel sprays its deadly rain around me: a Zeppelin makes vain attempts to place a bomb in my petrol tank & howitzers make fierce thrusts from every direction. Men fall in heaps on every hand, and clouds of poison gas envelop me – but scatheless I rush on, to hand the message over with a cheery smile & a request for a cigarette. <u>Do</u> I live a life fraught with danger?

We are now in a dug-out in the grounds of a château. I assure you it is some dug-out! We have a bedroom & a boudoir, both of vast extent; incidentally, there are three of us in it. I was much amused at your account of the beef trouble – buy an entrenching tool next time; they are invaluable for such cases, & make excellent egg-whisks or baby-soothers too.

Who told you about magnetos & so on? A girl of your age shouldn't know all that – it is neither right nor proper. But you got it correct, all the same. Please, please, don't apologise for the length of your letter – the longer the better! And the more of them the better! Only I hope you won't expect immediate answers, as I can't keep the war waiting while I write! The cards were a Godsend! I lost 6 francs 50 last night, &, having no more ready money went on to lose two buttons, a safety-razor blade (2nd hand) & a piece of soap (which didn't belong to me). Oh yes; thanks very much for the cards.

I am riding for the Artillery at present, though I still live with the old gang. It is only a temporary job, while one of their men is not fit. This is awful balderdash, but I hope you will excuse it! My brain is considerably impaired by the strain of continual shell fire! I've got to go & wash the baby now – so *à toi* – local colour.

Jack S. Riggs

The letter dated 13 August is written very neatly in pencil, and is more coherent and better punctuated than any of his previous ones. It is scarcely credible that the same person wrote the description of his despatch ride. Ed.

16 August, 1917

Dear Girl,

This isn't a letter, just a note with my address. If you have written to Base I'll have it in three or four days I expect. I arrived last night. Just before a "push" and was in the thick at 4 a.m. this morning with two howitzers. You may remember which I expected to go to, well these are larger, the same but larger 8 inch. I can't tell you a lot as we are still straffing and I have only a minute. Address is 239 Siege Battery B.E.F. and it's somewhere in <u>Belgium</u>

quite new for me. We are just north of a certain famous town. So you can guess. And if you see that we've been pushing at above date, you may get roughly there. Officers & Major in partic. are very decent. Major is an old regular ranker and seems hopeful he can teach me something. I warned him I knew nothing.

We had quite a decent joining up with most of the old K. squad. We were broken up at Rail head most of us going to different armies. No one in the battery has had leave yet but they haven't been out very long and there may be hopes when winter sets in. Anyhow I do want leave <u>now</u>. Can't really say much more. There's a horrid row going on and me poor head isn't used to it after "Blighty" for six months. I am wondering if you can read this. I bought a new pen in London and don't know if it writes better or worse.

Post is uncertain here I believe. Goes out at irregular hours & arrives ditto. When I get settled & a little peace I'll really write – at least I'll give it a try, because I find it hard to write. Hope the knee is progressing well. You'll have to be fit next time I'm back. I can't say any more just now. Do you still play <u>chess</u>?

Yours, John S. Riggs

Flanders 25 August, 1917

My dear Girl,

I wish I could hear from you. It's ages now and I've never had a letter yet. I hope it's just the post that's wrong & not anything to do with you. You know I'm getting more & more satisfied and content every time. I thought once that I would only worry but I don't somehow. I just know you and am sure things are right. Dear, I haven't much I can say till I hear from you. I admit it's not very nice waiting but I'm always hoping for the next day's post. So maybe it will be tomorrow. Say you <u>are</u> sure you still mean it. It seems too good to be true sometimes. I'm having quite a happy time. One of the officers here I knew at school, and my old division is only a few miles away. I went over to see them one afternoon. Panting came over to me this afternoon and I hope with his help to win a Triumph sometime. We have a car, a Clyno & sidecar, & two Douglas in the battery, but a Triumph would suit me much better than any. Every now & again the Major gives us a day off & we take the car for a joy ride to buy things for the mess. Oh, Panting wished to be remembered to you – he always said it would happen you know.

I'm just beginning to discover how good the time was I spent with you. I do love you girl. I don't believe I really told you before? Did I? Anyway you must have guessed fairly well. I have written twice before in case you didn't get my letters and address is 239 Siege Battery R.G.A., B.E.F. It's just possible that both my last letters went astray. How's the jolly old ring going on? I wish somehow you had got something that cost more. It seemed awful little for you, and I do like spending money for you.

Well *enfant* must go to sleep. Had a very easy day today. Last two or three days I was working as I was sent on ahead to take a new position and was on my own with two guns for some three days. Quite enjoyed myself. But I should have been rather lost if I hadn't been out before. Still I don't think the Major would have sent me if I hadn't.

Well cheerio girl dear, Yours John S. Riggs

Flanders 27 August, 1917

Dearest Girl,

I've had your two letters. The second one arrived first just as I was starting for 24 hours at O.P. so I took it along with me to console me. Strange to say it did & I spent quite a happy night. Your second & your Mother's & one from Nina & Ledlie were waiting for me when I got back. I've just had dinner & been packed off to bed by my Major. He's that sort. "Riggs I don't want to see you before 10 a.m. tomorrow" and off you've got to go. Will you excuse this being just a note as I'm rather weary.

Yes, I've got a tin hat. I don't wear it unless I go forward of course. In any case it's not the first one I've worn. You were correct as to the push. Just behind the place you mentioned. In fact I was watching what is left of the Church this morning. Your first letter to me was read in one of the old German strong points. You may have heard of them – about 4 ft of concrete all round so it is fairly safe.

Girl dear I do know how lucky I am. I told my friend James Henderson inside ten minutes of meeting him. We drank both your healths at Southampton. I'm sorry this writing isn't better only writing in bed is difficult. I'll write tomorrow & answer your letters. Only post goes early & I want you to get this as soon as possible. Dorothy I am caring more every day. I'm afraid you'll have an awful time when I get back again. I'm just beginning to realise things <u>are</u> true and not a dream. There are heaps of things I want to say but I'll have to postpone till tomorrow.

Cheerio girl dear, Yours
John S. Riggs

29 August, 1917

Dear Girl,

Just a note to let you know you aren't forgotten <u>yet</u>. And to enclose a note I got from Cpl Hobson of the 15th Div. The reference to J. Walker is "Johnnie Walker" a bottle of which I sent them. We came out together, about 30 all told, just in charge of ourselves, and <u>I</u> was quite well behaved. I haven't seen any Belgian girls yet, and won't round this way as they were cleared out. This pen is giving out. My letters are censored by me. I am the censor for my little mob. I'll write again tomorrow.

Cheerio, John S. Riggs

France, 1 September, 1917

My dear *mademoiselle* (local colour),

I beg to apologise most awfully humbly for not having answered your long screed before – if you only knew how busy we are you would be filled with pity rather than ire. It is now 17 days since I had time to eat anything, so you see I must be in a pretty bad way. But now I've really got several minutes leisure, so of course I hasten to get pencil & paper & begin this. [*This letter is written very neatly without any flourishes and scorings out which feature in some of the earlier ones written in ink with an italic nibbed pen.*] We are afflicted by weather – lots of it: we have been nearly snowed up for several days now, & two nights ago, I got lost in a blizzard, & found myself well behind the German lines. Hastily gathering a few scraps of information – all I could see lying around – I set my prismatic compass to mean Greenwich time & 'bout turned: just as the General was about to give me a spare V.C. he had in the office – I woke up & found I was late for the six o'clock parade!

Why do you assume that, because I have an extensive correspondence, I write to some "other girls"? May I point out that your remark has hurt my feelings very severely, & shattered my belief in mankind – before I got your letter, I should have said that no man would write to more than one girl at a time, except on business, but you from your experience, have taught me better. I should like you to understand that the bulk of my correspondence refers to the management of my estates in England, Ireland, Peru & Senegambia & is <u>all</u> addressed to agents of mine – male to a man. I shall be pleased to accept your apology.

Do you notice that I have had to adopt a new system of filing & numbering? I stopped the old straightforward method when I reached ten thousand. The rags you sent me are now in use as bedclothes at night, & puttees in the day time – the check puttee excites nearly as much admiration as the yellow one with the blue stripe: and they are beautifully warm at night.

Since you are so well up in the theoretical side of motor cycling, will you please explain why a magneto circuit cannot pass through a No. 38 jet except when counter impelled by a Dunlop super-armature generator? I should be much obliged if you could let me know, as I am much worried by the problem.

Dorothy on the Triumph

The cards are still going awfully strong – I am only a dog-biscuit & a broken mouth organ down on the last fortnight's play, so my game must be improving. I'm still a bit poor with my mashie shots, but my late cut & my long loser off the red are distinctly strong. If I ever win anything, I'll send it on to you (if it's no use to me).

There is very little news – I've only been wounded twice – I should let you know where, but the Censor might not appreciate it. I'm afraid this is very brief & disconnected. I have got to go up on duty very soon & have had no dinner yet – so cheery-ho.

Yours as ever, Jack S. Riggs

2 September, 1917

Dearest Girl,

I received your last two letters (28th & 29th) this afternoon. Many thanks *enfant*. And I think you should have had my note in answer to your first by now. I'm sorry I didn't know about your relations in Rouen. We stopped there only a day during which I fed & slept having nothing else to do. I'm sorry it's been so long. But I've written as often as I can, and you must curse the post. Letters are not as good as – chess? for instance. We have only one post a day and if there's nothing one just settles down to another 24 hours. I knew early there was one for me today & I felt certain it was from you. I was on the guns at the time firing, and the Sgt who was sorting the post passed and told me there was one. The rest of the battery have now come along so I'm free to be foolish once more. And <u>Don't</u> please put Flanders on my letters – you are not supposed to know I'm there. Really you are a most impatient young lady. Yes, perhaps you are a lady – I have never pretended to be a gentleman, and am only lending civilian assistance to the Army!

Dear Girl I do not bark. I may speak crossly, but the Sgts or Sgt Major do the barking. There is usually not much need as the work isn't really hard. I'm writing about 10.15 p.m. in my bunk. Very fine night. Old Archie is banging away at Fritz overhead, but neither ever do any real harm. Archie is an optimist. He always misses and yet cheerfully starts firing again next time. "Hope springs . . ." I went over to see the 15th people before they left for a rest the other day. Hobson tried to crow over me but he didn't really succeed. Panting and Norris (the artificer) are the only original ones. Cameroon Berry was killed. He was R.F.A. I showed Pant & Hobo one of your photos. I don't think I should tell you what they said or you will get conceited. – to the effect that I always was lucky.

The Douglas aren't much good. Nevertheless as they are cheap they are supplied more easily than Triumph. And as there are enormous numbers of poor riders its as well they are. I've found a Triumph and have just been fixing her up a little to suit my own taste. My dear Girl! Sure people knew as soon as they saw a handsome young man like me that you would lose your head (and heart?) at once! Bound to. Dorothy – oh yes – you seem to have doubts miss as to whether you'll marry me or not. Well let me tell you you'll find it difficult to escape now. Sure I'd be after leave to come & marry you now if I thought you'd alter your mind! So be careful *enfant*!

I'm sorry to disappoint you, but I'm right about the size. You may not have heard of them (I hadn't myself) but they are there all right.* As I've told you in a previous note I am my own censor unless they are reopened at the Base. Doesn't often happen so – you are correct in thinking I wouldn't be quite so friendly in a few of my statements. Glad you liked *Valley of the Moon*. I am sorry to hear about your knee – please be gentle on it. I think I'd rather like to see you in rags! Does your hair come down then? And I suppose rags means silk stockings etc. I'm sorry you are broke. Can I return many kind offers to me and lend you 2/6. But honestly I'd like to get you something cos I've heaps of money. I've got my back pay from the Engineers – some £20. Would you get shoes, hats or rags or stockings if I send you some? Will you let me girl? Please. Well if I [*quadruple underlined*] marry you I'll give you all the cash I've got. I never do know how much and where, so I might just as well. And you'll likely lose it. That is one thing I can do – lose money cheerfully. Of course I don't dare suggest that household necessities are loss, but you know what I mean. Art supplement indeed! About knees: I rather like them myself – you have suffered & should know. I'd rather have your lips just now.

Dorothy dearest, Goodnight,

Yours most certainly, John S. Riggs

* *Howitzers?*

4 September, 1917

Dearest Girl,

I haven't really anything much to say. I'm just writing "all for the love of you" and it won't be long. I may be posted to another battery tomorrow or a day later – 145 Siege I think. Uncertain as yet.

You said in your first letter "if you ever do feel lonely". I used to but not now. I do know that you <u>are</u> there & things aren't nearly so bad then. I notice by the way Miss Kendall that you are adopting a very didact tone about what you'll allow me to do & what not. I think you're a bully! But I rather like being bullied by you.

I'll enclose a note for Barbara [*Hanna, best friend from Richmond Lodge school*] with this. Explain won't you how awfully busy I am with the war & the way Haig trusts me to carry out all his really big pushes! I'm afraid I hurt Barbara's feelings once when she asked me to that dance. I didn't mean to, but Nina hinted that I had. You see *enfant*, I'm not given to saying polite things (as you know). Of course since <u>you</u> took me in hand I've improved lots. Oh yes I have, I'm sure of it. Maybe if I marry you you might be quite a success.

Well *enfant*, must sleep, goodnight Dorothy,
John S. Riggs

6 September, 1917

Dorothy dear,

Just a line. I have altered my address and though there is just a chance of my going back to the last battery my address at present is 145 Siege Battery R.G.A. At present we are having 5 days rest – at least the rest of the battery is, but I haven't reached the Rest Camp yet. That's where the Triumph comes in. I can move about on my own and go round to see my friends. I slept at this place last night and am writing after breakfast. No one here except some men left as a guard. Still I'm quite happy & they put me up quite well. I hope to reach the next camp today sometime – I'm sending my kit along and I'll follow if I find nothing better to do. I can promise you though that I won't give any glad eyes. I don't like the girls you may come across, and they are few and far between. You see when I had you meet me I could afford to be reckless as I'm certain you would protect me. But by myself it's a different matter. I really must clear off & see about my kit.

Cheerio enfant darling, John S. Riggs

France, Saturday night, 17 September

Dear Girl,

This <u>must</u> be a note. It's 11.50 p.m. & I was up all last night. My address is again 28 Siege Battery R.G.A. After much trouble the Major (seeing the staff about once a day) got me back again. Porton? The other man who was transferred, who I knew at school, hasn't got back. I moved down for a rest in a quiet sector for a time. Quite nice around here – hardly hear a gun & very decent roads.

I saw my old Div. again today. They are back in the position they were in when I was at home. They're also for rest. That is of course no active fighting. It does not mean out of the line. I haven't heard from anyone for nearly a week. Expect they'll all come in a bunch. Must sleep. I'll write you properly when I get time.

Yours, John S. Riggs

France 14 September, 1917

Dorothy dear,

I have two letters of yours to answer. And two parcels of food & books came yesterday too. I couldn't write at once because I was on O.P. when I got your first & on duty with the forward section when I got yesterday's three all at once. Nearly as good as leave. Someway I knew there would be a letter for me on the 12th (that was the day I was on O.P. & you do 24 hours) and I sent a man down to the letters to get it. There were three, one from you, one from your mother & one from Nina.

I can't really answer just now as I'm writing outside the B.C. post and don't like spreading several dozen sheets of paper round me. One might blow away. It's nearly 7 p.m. and I'll wait till after dinner.

Many thanks for your books. I've read *The 39 Steps* already. It's not as you say very good, but still it's something to read. The other I haven't looked at yet but I have a faint idea I read it before. Or was it another of the same title by Barry Pain – I can't remember till I read it again. You're quite a good girl sometimes. The envelopes you enclose come in very useful & it was <u>thoughtful</u> (I'm sure you'll hate the word!) of you to send them. You see nearly all the envelopes get stuck down with the all pervading moisture and a few fresh ones that aren't are welcome.

I think I have written two notes that you hadn't got when you wrote. They'll tell you that I did go to the other battery & then the major got me back. I'm very glad, both because I knew & liked the people & also that this battery was going to a quiet sector for a rest & the other wasn't. It's beautifully peaceful here. It's where there was a decent push when I was home, and as a result the after effect is quietness. Hardly ever hear a shell. Major goes on leave in a day or two. It's a start anyway, though there are five still to go before me. I'm last of course.

The Captain here & myself were just discussing fitting up electric light. The difficulty is to win a dynamo somewhere. He suggests getting one sent out but that doesn't seem the thing quite.

Our forward section here is billleted in what was once a very decent château. Fritz has made strong concrete places in it, but there is one small room on the ground floor nearly intact. Leastways intact enough to sleep in.

Quite like home. There was a decent garden & staircase, fruit trees etc.

After 11 p.m. This was intended to be a really long letter but it's getting late now and I must be up early tomorrow. I'm writing in bed having just got there. Hobson didn't say a lot. I think he felt it useless. No, there weren't any bets on but I used to rag him & Panting for not being free. Quite good natured you know. But Hobo always used to say wait my boy. Well, as I used to point out to him it wasn't what I would do in the future I never pretended I wouldn't be some time. I knew such a fine young man as I was was bound to be snapped up! Yes, Cameroon Berry went to Field Artillery.

I'm afraid I'm fed up tonight, I don't know why. Only well I want you & (poor thing) he can't get what he wants! I'll just cry. I haven't looked at your first letter again to answer – I'll keep that till later. You've made the remark (twice I think) that it's nice to be able to write as often as you want without exciting coment. Do you by any chance mean that you did want to before? It doesn't seem possible to me that you should care for comment – you don't profess to.

I was afraid you wouldn't like me to send anything or I would have sent at once without asking. Maybe that would have got me my way all right but I'd rather ask you first. I'll think about keeping it later. One can't find much here. How long do you think I'd have to keep it. Remember I'm not good at keeping money.

Did you ever read *The Seats of the Mighty* by Sir Gilbert Parker. There are some verses in it starting 'Oh Flower of all the world . . .' that keep running in my head & I can't remember them all. See if you can find them for me will you *enfant*. Oh, I think your quotation about a pretty wit & a pretty pretty wit is from *The Yeoman of the Guard,* isn't it by the Jailor when he's remarking on his stories of torture etc. to the Jester. Maybe I'm wrong & you're thinking of something else. I'll get this off tomorrow morning. Our post always leaves in the morning & arrives with the rations about tea time (with luck).

Good night enfant dear,
John S. Riggs

France, 15 September, 1917

Dorothy dear,

This is in answer to yours of the 3rd Sept. They have been answered backwards, but I don't suppose you'll mind a fearful lot. No, the major does not go the lengths you mention. He contents himself with "good night" and doesn't even see me off the step! Besides even if he did he has an enormous waist. (What's that got to do with it?) Really, you know, the information you require! I can't tell you all the details. Sometimes the O.P. stunt is quite interesting, but others rotten. When its raining or misty & you can't see a yard & yet must stop there it becomes an awful war. Sometimes (not often) quite exciting. Yes of course you're a very clever girl, and charming. I've been putting the pretty pink stamp, as you call it, on about 200 to 300 letters today & I'm sick of it. It happened that all the other men were out & so I got the whole lot to do. Usually we each do our own sections.

Have just heard (as I'm orderly officer today & tonight I hear all these things first) that we are to get another officer to take Poston's place.

The liquid we drank your health in was the best champagne we could get. Then we went & sent telegrams. I like you asking questions – even silly ones – shows you take a little interest which I'm not very used to. Did I ever say that I <u>objected</u> to your giggle. I called it inane etc. & lectured about it, but I'm sure I never objected. I say & said heaps of things that you very well know I don't mean.

Will you tell your mother I'll write as soon as possible. Of course she'll understand that <u>you must</u> come first? Honestly though girl, I want to know something: that is if you can tell me just when you were sure you wanted me. Was it when I was at Bexhill or when I was back on that last 10 days. Because I had decided when I left for Bexhill not to come home again if I could get straight out, at least not to see you again. And then you wrote & said something about being more than a friend. So I thought I'd chance it once more cursing meself for a fool all the time. You know I found it very hard to believe you did mean it & were not just being bullied into it. I tried (at times!) to leave you alone (which was what really made me so bad tempered) and let you decide. I look on things very differently now to the last time. I have something now & I'm counting on it. I want to talk to you again about this subject. I'm full of desire to know what little things everything turns on. An hour here and perhaps a word there – and it's settled.

I haven't much longer to write as the other officers will be turning up shortly. I'm glad to hear the old knee is going on all right. Only see & don't crock up again trying to work. I'm just looking forward to your next letter. That's the worst of just having had one, you can't expect another for a week. Still you've been awfully good & written really often. I'll think of a suitable reward for you. I must really stop although I could go on like this for ages just saying nothing – still they are from France the magic B.E.F. and suppose will have that much interest. You haven't decided what you are going to be married in have you? It might be as well to have at least one frock that would serve, or are you waiting so you'll be in the latest fashion.

Cheerio girl dearest.

Yours John S. Riggs

21 September, 1917

Dorothy dear,

Now then Miss Cheekiness! I've been writing to several people & left you to the last. No I'll write you another note. I nearly always leave your letters to be read last & I like to write you last. I've just made a frantic hunt for a letter dated 8th Sept. I had the 7th & wonder if you wrote again. It's all right because it was posted on the 8th.

You will have had my note announcing my change back again to 239 Siege. Your letter I've just had was addressed on, which accounts for the delay because – please excuse candle grease, it just toppled over – we moved south and it always means delay when you move. This is a district I've never been in before, and is quite interesting as there was a push here while I was home. We are quite well off for billets & there's a decent sized town where we can get plenty of provisions not far away. We aren't having a war really round this way. Quite peaceful and topping weather. Also I can see me old friends as they are quite handy. They know this country of course & can tell me where to look for things. Most awful – you may remember me telling you of a man who was arrested for looting in A . . . Well he got off all right & is now in England for commission. Ledlie is very keen to know what I write you. I've told her there isn't much, but I'm afraid she doesn't believe me.

I don't think I'm getting <u>much</u> thinner. A little perhaps, but there's still the winter & I want a good coating of fat to last me! So please don't say off just yet. I can't and won't run miles just to get thin to please you. Not with winter coming. I'm writing about 9 p.m. while waiting for a "how" to come along. I'm in charge of the forward section for the last four days. Relieved tomorrow. Then . . . Cheerio.

Yours John S. Riggs

30 September, 1917

Dear Girl,

I have two letters of yours to answer. I doubt if either will be answered tonight as I'm on O.P. and I can't spread your letter about here – also one is liable to be interrupted at any moment. Your first letter I had when on the other O.P. (we have several) and the second when with the forward section. I haven't really had time the last week to write. You see there were two on leave & two away (one on a course & one on rest camp). The result was the remainder got rather a lot to do. Still one doesn't grouse when it's caused by leave. Otherwise they might say well you can't send so many & that would be awful. I liked your second letter awfully. I notice you've dropped the <u>if</u> I marry you & now seem determined about it. I'm afraid I'll be bullied but I don't really mind. Rather like it I think – leastways sometimes.

I've been on this job two days & yesterday evening Hobson came along to see me. The brigade he's with at present isn't far away & I had sent a note to him. I gave him your messages. Oh did I tell you that Panting has gone home to get married at last. He got special leave first & went off in great excitement I believe. We intend to go round & blackmail him *après la guerre* cos I'm sure Mrs Panting has a great idea of him & we know him very well. Thank heaven he doesn't know anything he could blacken my character with.

Your imagination as to my whereabouts isn't far out. Of course I can't say where! Anyway I don't think it would convey anything. I know your feeling nevertheless. It's 9 p.m. and I'm very sleepy. No real reason to be because I had at least six hours last night. But I miss me bed. You can't you know bring it along – awful pity! My <u>dear</u> girl you are <u>always</u> silly, otherwise you wouldn't be you. Why make excuses for it?

At present I overlook the river S . . . and it's tempting in day time (It's quite hot at times) to go down & have a swim only Fritz might object. I'm afraid I can't find much more to say. It's a glorious moonlight night, and if it wasn't so chill would be most enjoyable. My fat will be useful yet. Must leave this, good-night girl dearest.

John S. Riggs

4 October, 1917

Dearest,

Cheer up I still love you! I can't write you a long letter to <u>prove</u> it just now, and I might have difficulty in so doing. Still believe me this time.

I have three of your letters to answer when I get the chance. Meanwhile be good & get the knee better. Have you seen the doc. again or are you just carrying on. I'm sure you must have done more than ride a motor to do all that damage. Do you know what really did it? Jolly old war is still going on. I'm just off on the bus to draw money to pay the battery. Like to come? Roads aren't as good as they might be of course, and you'd have to ride behind. No, I think you'd better not come in <u>person</u>. I'll likely look round & see Hobson and some others on my way back. Last time I was there two had just returned from a joy ride to A . . . a place I used to visit when on the Somme. One was left on the road while the other did 20 kilos or so for a new axle for the side car wheel. Now I never let that happen. Anyway the man who came back did it on the sidecar machine which they detached, and the point of the yarn I'm coming to is he "put it across" a Yank on one of their far-famed Indians. Makes us quite happy.

Well *enfant* must go. Cheerio.
Yours John S. Riggs

12 October, 1917

Dearest,

I'm not going to answer either of your last two tonight. I'm rather weary having been out all day. Really nothing doing only the air makes me sleepy. I've been on O.P. in horrid wet rain and am writing in my bunk about 10 p.m. I've installed a stove (made from a 5 gallon oil drum) which is most comforting. I like stoking fires & when I give my <u>undivided</u> attention to it am very good at it.

Haddon (he's a schoolmaster in civvie life) & I share the bunker. A new one we had built as we were turned out of our first to make a kitchen. I'll draw a little plan. You understand it's dug into the bank on the roadside. I'll let you know about improvements as we get them in. No, I haven't read Serentien[?]. As far as I know unless it appeared in Nash's as monthly instalments. Many thanks indeed for verses. I'm glad you liked them too. I've remembered them since I first read "The Feet of the Mighty".

No, you never just said you were lonely: I thought you might be a little and get over it. I didn't expect you would still. Cheer up girl dear. I'll get leave sometime I hope. I told you in my last letter how things were. And I can be lonely too! This afternoon on the O.P. I dozed off (I had oilskins & rubber boots so was dry enough) & I had nice visions of you for 5 or 10 minutes.

I notice your threats about "<u>if</u> I marry you" have stopped. Decided now? I think I'll risk the cooking. You see if you do make a howler I could just take over & show you myself! I'm not really in a writing mood. I'm not very often which explains why you don't get longer letters, and I must write home as they have "sent a parcel".

Yours *enfant* dear, John S. Riggs

13 October, 1917

Dear Dorothy,

I have just read your letter dated 5/10. Many 'fanks'. I'm writing again in our bunk having just succeeded in having a bath. Rather a job in a couple of gallons. Anyhow that's over and our old stove is roaring away & we've got a real thick atmosphere. We must all be up early tomorrow so I'm going to retire early. It's about 9.50 p.m. now. Oh, alright, I'll be quite good in case you change your mind. Still I feel you know a good thing when you've got it!? And it's not necessary to use force to be a bully. There are all sorts. I don't think that you will really treat me very badly. I'll chance it anyway.

Dorothy! I am astonished at you. Really I thought you knew how good I always am too well to hint that there might be things Pant didn't know of. He finds out most things & you can depend on it if <u>he</u> doesn't know there isn't anything to know. Now miss!

We aren't really cold yet. Only wet so far, and we aren't out more than we can help as you·may guess. I'm sorry *enfant* it was so long since you had a letter. You see a day slides past very quickly & unless you make up your mind to do such a thing at a certain time, it's as if bed first & everything else last. I carried your letter round all day from about 10 a.m. this morning (slight pause to stoke fire) meaning to read it & answer tonight. I'm seldom too pushed to write but I want to write as long letters as possible & so I often wait till I can spend as long as I want over it.

We started playing cards this afternoon in the B.C. post (that is Battery Commander's Post – where the battery is fought from). I installed a stove there & it's a very popular place just now. You see there has to be an officer on duty there always & it's usually the last place to find anyone else. It's different now with the stove. But about cards. You'll have to hurry with that stocking – I lost 2 francs. Bang went sixpence! Awful life a gambler's. In the midst of it the colonel walked in & there was a hurried scramble! Oh I meant to ask you would a khaki silk muffler be any good to you. I'm afraid that's the only colour. I can get what are said to be fairly good ones. I'll send it along anyway & you can cut it up for something else if it's no good. Oh & when just is your birth-day. I know you've told me several times, but I forget the exact date.

Somewhere near Xmas isn't it? ("Doesn't look as if he <u>really</u> loves me not knowing when my birthday is.") But I do and you'll be 21 then. Awful! Beginning to get sense perhaps. Worse still! Well I must roll in. I'll write you again sometime Dorothy dear. You are a good kid & when she likes <u>quite</u> charming.

Good night my dearest.
John S. Riggs

16 October, 1917

Dear old girl,

Your letter & book arrived yesterday. Many thanks and – – – (you can fill in the blank?!) The book was very welcome as I hadn't anything to read & I was for duty today with our forward section. It's rather nice here as you are on your own & nothing to do or worry about. The only trouble is I do <u>sometimes</u> get tired of my own company. I'm writing about 9 p.m. in my bunk in the château. (It's a ruined village we are in). I haven't as yet started to answer your letter. It's just your own dear foolishness of course. Oh, about that scarf. It hasn't gone yet as I'm hunting for a suitable box to pack it in.

Alright, I don't believe the old motor hurt the knee myself. Because you wouldn't use a knee grip on that crock & besides you haven't learnt the need for one yet. You will some day we'll hope. And then you'll likely break your neck. Never mind you can only die once! Re Expedition to A . . . Not the place you thought, further back. The D.R. knew it was a Yank because only they use Indians, and their uniform is different. It's not altogether a silly question! You seem rather fearful of asking silly questions. Sure you must learn & I like to encourage you. You'll soon be quite clever!

Re Carrier. I hae me douts if you could stick on. I know I shouldn't like to risk it side-saddle, and I'm sure you are too still too much a lady to ride astride.

I was off again yesterday to draw more money. Coming back had quite a good speed burst with a R.F.S. on a P. & M. (you know the R.F.C. use P. & M.?) The roads in the back areas are really quite good. Quite as good as at home and in places better. It's forward, they have such a lack of knowledge of a road's duties.

I <u>did</u> reply re your frock two letters back. I doubt if we'll ever get a real Rugger match. You see nearly all the men play Soccer and it's almost impossible to raise a XV. Still when we get the footer togs out from England we'll have a try. We travel back of course when we do play a match. Even the "feel" of a Rugger ball is good for me.

I have exhausted my supply of wood for the stove here. It's a French one belonging to the château. You know I have ideas meself as to houses and one relates to fires. I think the usual type of fireplace is a most wasteful affair besides only getting one front. In plan and section it's usually built into the wall, but you would get far more heat if you built out from the wall. The French nearly all adopt the last method, usually a large metal affair and they certainly make heat.

LA GUERRE DANS LE NORD
21 VERMELLES — L'Entrée du Village - La troisième barricade

542

Postcard sent by Jack

I've had a letter from V. Menary [*Vera?*] today, been following me all over the place as she put the wrong number. I'll bet she's swearing never to write again because I haven't answered. Oh Dorothy dear I'm still losing money! Awful game "pontoon". Someone <u>must</u> love me to account for my horrible luck. You know "lucky in love, unlucky at cards". Leastways so I console meself!

There's a large rat working away in the corner here & keeping an eye on me. Cleared off now. Well girl dear I have exhausted all I can say. Oh – did I tell you I'm growing a moustache! How would <u>you</u> like that? It is only to save meself trouble of course and I can promise it will come off at once when I get leave! At present I get an extra minute in bed o'mornings. Must say good night dearest.

Yours John S. Riggs

17 October, 1917

Dear Dorothy,

Just a line to keep you happy. I'm sure a letter of mine will clear away the blackest of household worries. Poor *enfant*! I haven't anything to say really and I haven't an envelope to put this in – hoping for some in the morning.

We had a Frenchman round here today who used to live here. I told you we were in the remains of W . . . Been quite a decent little village in its time. Anyway he came round (while on leave) to see the place. I guess it must look strange to him. I went round with him while he showed me where he used to live.

I have used nearly all the wood for my fire. When the last bit goes on I go to bed. I expect to get the engine of my bus down tomorrow and grind valves in etc. – think you could do it? It wouldn't take me long to show you. Leastways on second thoughts it would! Difficult things motor cycle engines!

I hear you're making another blouse. Do you give them all names – like the fashion plates do? Oh, I've discovered a hole in one sock! At the heel – that's the result of wearing those rubber boots. They wear out your socks so quick – still they save a minute or two in dressing. I'm writing as usual on me bed, and watching the old fire – that's the last of the wood gone on. Say this is an awful daft letter isn't it?

I've a bet with the last "sub" here that the war won't be over by Xmas. He says it will. Optimist that's £5 in my pocket. What would you like? Anything! Nice little car for that price? No? Well chum dear, I must turn in. I told your mother about this general after my job tomorrow. Must get my tin hat freshly trimmed. Quite mad! Are you still determined to marry me? Remember how young you are! I remember two letters back you called <u>me ME</u> pie-face. Right you'll get kissed hard for that – and oftener than you like. Good night Dorothy.

J. S. R.

19 October, 1917

Dorothy dear,

Really nothing at all to write about. The general hasn't turned up yet to take my job. He could have it with pleasure if I could go home. I haven't heard from you for ages, nearly <u>three days</u>! It's enough to make any self respecting person stop loving you! I'm afraid I haven't much self respect though.

I'm getting awful bored with myself. I haven't anything except "Red" mags & that sort to read, and one does get tired of that high class printing matter (you can't call it anything else). Augh me. It's a weary world. Why can't you come out and hold me hand. How's the old knee. You really must get it better. Can't you try Christian Science or something. "Something" I'm sure would be good for it. I'm fed up tonight: not really you know but just wanting something to do. Only thing is bed and it's only about 9 – rather early but little boys should be in bed early.

Well goodnight enfant dearest.
Yours always, John S. Riggs

22 October, 1917

Dorothy dearest,

I've had your letter dated 13th since day before yesterday, but I've been on O.P. since and no chance to write. It's 10 p.m. now and I must rise me early in the morn, so this will only be a note. I hope to add a line or two tomorrow before the mail goes as I'll have to relieve a man for breakfast, and while waiting for him may get a few minutes quiet. That's the real difficulty with me.

I can't write letters with lots of people running in and out. Haddon who shares the bunk with me is the same way, so we retire together when we can to write. Doesn't look so unsociable when two of us clear out.

I don't want to marry you for your household abilities. You quite seem to think I do, and there isn't any "have to" please. I never have any socks mended thank you – wear them till the end & then throw them away. Much simpler. Haddon has just written you a note. I have warned him not to write a letter card (he always does), but I expect he will just the same. Re stockings: I don't remember seeing <u>you</u> wearing pink & yellow stripes & green spots somehow – and it was one of yours that was required. I'm certain it won't be filled with much except the dirty little French notes for 2.5d. & 5d. they are so fond of issuing. Mr Cox (nice man) looks after the more solid part of the job. So maybe even one with a hole might do. Though I don't promise to leave <u>much</u> money in it. The colour I think had better be left to you, you are bound to know more about it than me!

Well I'm awful sleepy, *enfant*. Will finish tomorrow I hope. How will you have managed to exist without a letter for two days?! I think I'm awful good, considering it's me. Do you remember a time when I didn't write for about three months & you'd given up any expectation of hearing again. I don't think you guessed at all what your letters ment [*sic*] to me on more than one occasion. And you were far too kind when I did get home. I couldn't help loving you straight away. <u>Must</u> say good night.

Goodnight dearest, John S. Riggs

23 October, 1917

Dear Girl,

I'm sorry but I can't write this morning. Keep having to run out for something. I'm just scribbling this before the mail goes, so that you won't expect one. Horrid wet day.

Cheerio, write later, John S. Riggs

24 October, 1917

Dearest,

I have two more of your letters to answer. One dated 16th & t'other 17th. First to finish off the 13th one. Re. Negatives you are quite correct – that's what happened – only don't worry to send any prints. I've seen them, thanks just the same for the ones you did send. Yes Mother I believe always tells the story of the vegetable marrow & the railway. It's rather beginning to get whiskers, but never mind. I don't know of course what she tells. I only know what happened – I was blamed as usual. Though for the life of me I can't see how I was to know she was in the habit of carrying jam pots – full – in her personal kit. Will you tell Rosemary [*Dorothy's sister – 13 years younger*] I'll send a button as soon as I can find one.

You seem to have been hit by the remark that you might be called clever. Sure you know *enfant* I do think you are <u>quite</u> clever. Only I can't tell you so too often or you'll get so proud you won't speak to me. We don't use candles as a rule. The acetylene generator of my bike is rigged up as a gas meter. Much better than a candle! We've only two looking glasses. Mirror-shaving 2 of, but the clock & china dogs (the usual isn't it?) we hope to "win" some day.

Your letter dated 17th came this morning. I'm pleased my humble efforts keep you cheerful. I'll try & keep it up, though I just write when I can & when I feel like it. Right again – Miss Kendall – you keep an open mind! Only you must be prepared to suffer for it. You <u>may</u> be quite right. Only – proof? And about the oil-drum, it is about 20 inches by ten. You first cut out the top (so it's got the bung hole in it) and punch it full of holes for a grate; then you cut nicks (about three) in the sides of the drum & round it so you push the top inside & bend in the nicks. This makes a triangular hole on the grate level, so then you cut out a door above the grate & one below for ashes and lastly you cut a hole for a flue pipe. [*All this is illustrated*] It's cut in segments like this only the straight lines being cut. Then when you bend each segment out you have a good surface to join the pipe on to. See? Awful lot of piffle isn't it Dorothy. I've spent too long on that silly old stove. Must finish your letter later – it's 11 p.m. now.

Good night Girl dearest, John S. Riggs

28 October, 1917

Dear Dorothy,

Just a note to assure you I'm still living. The post goes in a few minutes. I received your last letter dated Oc. 20 and hope to answer it tonight. I expect to be going on a short course (5 days) so there may be a slight delay in my letters (or yours). Still the same address as it's not very far – I'll tell you more later. The "whiskers" I thought I told you it was only temporary, you can rest assured of that. I can't write just now – people keep running in & out. I'm in the B.C. post. Till later.

Cheerio, John S. Riggs

29 October, 1917

Dearest Girl,

I have received your last letter dated Oct. 1 yesterday. Many thanks. There are still two of your last ones to be answered but I must let you know I'm still alive & pleased to have your letters. In reply to yours of the 18/9/17 (the very large one in the big envelope): No, the second book you sent wasn't one I'd read. I only thought I had & thought wrong (for once, <u>even</u> the best make mistakes!). And I was certain you wouldn't like being called "thoughtful". Electric light cannot now be obtained from French mains as we have advanced beyond them. The time we got it was before the pushes & therefore we were still in civilisation. See?

1 started writing this before going to bed, but am going to continue in bed. For warmth! It begins to get rather cold o'nights. One drawback of writing often is that I lose what I was thinking in my letter & after I've written two or three times I get your reply to mine. Rather sad, but still I can bear up. Yes, I think I'd prefer the stocking! Maybe you could spare one & I'll see how full it won't get! The dress you describe & enclose a cutting of sounds well & I'm sure would look fine, especially if I saw you inside it. And I'm not bored by your dress talk. Perhaps <u>sometimes</u> I'll just grunt (that seems usually the way. Are you prepared?) Oh yes I read your mother's books. I'm sorry I forgot to mention that I had. I will when I write again. My only excuse is I read them on the journey over & somehow you don't seem quite disconnected from people till you stop & settle in a place. So I thought you were still with me in a way. Well I've been right through your large letter & I haven't really written much. Re my remarks as to what I'd like. Just you that's all.

Dear, dear girl, I would like to have treated you better and of course you'll say you told me to, but really I didn't cheer up much on the Downpatrick road did I? Chief thing I remember is kissing you. Still you knew I wouldn't behave roughly to you again. I don't quite know why I did. I told you once I wanted to hurt you at times & it must have been that. Yes, I think with luck I'll get leave about Xmas. There are two on leave now & two more before me. Of course you must be three months in the country before you are due. Still you can have all your frocks ready by then & I'll tell you how charming you look in each. Time goes on and I <u>must</u> be early tomorrow morning. Only 10 minutes for breakfast as the major likes us all on parade. So good [night] enfant darling. I'll write again soon. You are a good kid at times you know. Good night dearest.

Yours, John S. Riggs

2 November, 1917

Dear Girl,

I received your last yesterday. It was forwarded on to me here, which I didn't expect. I can't write at this time o'day. It's <u>war</u> and the post goes at 11 a.m. I'm at 13 Squadron R.F.C. at present having a great time. Nothing to do all day except hang round waiting for some pilot to take me up. It's great, and I quite think I should be in it . . .

I'm glad you liked the scarf – I was afraid the colour wouldn't suit, and it was the only one possible to get.

I expect to be returning to the battery in another day or two so you needn't alter the address. The gentleman with whom I share the bunker (a pilot named Davies) has just flung a paper at me – must go & deal with him. It will have to be gently as I hope he'll take me a joy ride this afternoon – – – he's gone out now! Well I haven't really answered your letter yet. I have two as a matter o'fact. Because the last one was only replied to with a note. I was moved off here rather hurriedly after being told I wasn't going and had given up hope. This isn't much of a letter, but I really will write soon. Till then bear up!

Re names. Very well. You call me what you like only don't blame me for what happens. Do you remember I suggested hung head down over a slow & <u>very</u> smoky fire. Well something like that. Dorothy you <u>are</u> clever. Yes, I mean it. Not pulling your leg this time. Quite correct about _____ . Reason the censor stamp was changed is just that every so often they do change them. Just as a check & to prevent things happening. Alright! I shan't ask any more. Only you brought it on yourself by starting "if" ing. I'm sorry to hear you've a cold. It's very clear you want your mother or someone to look after you. How's the knee this weather? Better I hope. Well I must toddle off with this. Also I hear aero engines! Must run!

Yours ever, John S. Riggs

4 November, 1917

My girl,

Just read your last letter dated 26/10/17. Many thanks. And also for the book which came same time, <u>and</u> a letter from your mother.

Well I've returned to the battery now and have quite enjoyed the R.F.C. stunt. I think I'll apply for it. Advantages are fairly numerous. First means most likely you go to England for a month's course as observer. Then about 4 months here & then back for another 4 months. You can count on leave about every 4 months I believe. The leave or chance of it has a great infuence on me! I should most likely be with an artillery squadron and their risks are not so tremendous. I'm sure I should like the job well. At least for a time! Re Haddon's note. No, I don't think I was particularly "fed up" – not above the normal. You do get a sort of fed-upness that's always there, but you derive a sort of pleasure from it. Haddon isn't in the bunker tonight. He's on duty in the B.C. post & I'm alone in me glory. I'll give him your note in the morn. If you've been cheeky about me in it – well I won't threaten any more. Action! No, I wasn't going to try not writing again. I want yours too much.

You really are a dear girl you know. Oh about your last remark saying that you thought I hoped you wouldn't marry me – you had better not think any such thing or you'll get married at once. And then what would you do!?

Dorothy dear I don't want you to send improving books just because they are. Things you've read yourself or that you think I'd like. Oh! I got a game of Rugger at the Squadron. It was quite good enough. Heavens I'm getting an old man! Soon be toddling round on two sticks. The R.F.C. played a Gunnery team, I played for the F.C. Gunners won by a goal & three tries to a goal (mine). [*Dorothy was not enchanted by the game and suffered from chronic chilblains.*]

I'm still not finished as I must soon go to bed. It is 10.30 & I'm up early tomorrow. I would like you to kiss me goodnight – even if you can't cook! I'm sad to hear from your mother that your knee went again. I'll have to attend to that myself I think. (Always do a job yourself if you want it done well!) So pleased you <u>rather</u> like me. I half hoped you did you know! Well *enfant* dearest I must toddle. I'll write as soon as I can again.

Oh if I apply for R.F.C. before this month is out I might get home for Xmas, otherwise it's more likely to be much later. There are still two to go. And I do want you near again girl. Goodnight chum dearest.

John S. Riggs

6 November, 1917

Dearest Girl,

Your last letter was waiting for me when I returned from the O.P. this morning. Many thanks. I'm not answering it now – tomorrow. I'm forward now in the village château I mentioned. *Compre?* And it's late. This is just a note.

Oh I read your book in the O.P. nursing an old grey cat that turned up. I thought it was rather (the book I mean) far fetched. Makes me feel cross when people are blind to chances. Now you couldn't complain I was! It is 10.30 p.m. and I have to do a practice turn out tonight. Or rather tomorrow morning. I'll make it about 3 a.m. I think. To see how long it takes to get the guns going in case of attack you know. Like a fire brigade we are! Well I hope to write you tomorrow. Oh I've sent for a form for the R.F.C. You'll let me won't you? See what I'm reduced to! Anyway you can believe me that I don't consider it any more risk than this. And this is fairly cushy. I can't explain the R.F.C. formation but coming from artillery means rather nice work.

I <u>still</u> love you, *enfant*, goodnight, John S. Riggs

7 November, 1917

Dorothy dear,

I guess I haven't much to say really but I said I would write & I'm not going to disappoint you – you are too good a kid. I've been reading all your letters you've written me here and wondering how to carry them all. They would certainly stop any bullet if there were any flying about. And paper is said to be a protection against the mustard gas! Oh, I gave Haddon your note & he showed it me next morning. Really Dorothy you'll get smacked! You will. I won't be able to control myself. Me blood boils now!

I think I was saying something about your last book which I didn't finish owing to interruptions. I thought the Bachelor was rather overdrawn. I don't think anyone could be quite so helpless. Oh, I had a letter from Percy Story (you may know his sister – she married a curate) today. He's in the Navy. He wrote wishing me luck etc. Nina had told his sister. How these things go round. I'm sorry I can't explain about films now. I will sometime later if you still want to know. I've already asked Gertie to get me a pair of Rugger boots <u>&</u> sent the cash. Most important from Gertie's point of view. Last time I played in borrowed ones too small for me & was a cripple afterwards. I had Rosemary's letter today. I'll send a P.C. but I couldn't write, besides the poor child couldn't read my scrawl anyway. I don't think the bunker will be improved much more now. We have a fairly comfy hole & that's enough. You will have to come along yourself. Sure. You <u>would</u> be welcome. You are a darling girl. I wish this old war would hurry up & finish. You know I don't see any end & I get impatient! Well *enfant* dear I'm getting silly. Before I get more so, Goodnight dearest.

Yours, John S. Riggs

9 November, 1917

Dearest Girl,

Yours of the 2nd just arrived. It's very late. Usually the mail comes in the morning but it didn't today. And yet I expected to hear from you before I went to bed. And it came along with tomorrow's orders. (You see a man goes down every night to our rear position for the next day's orders & I told him to get <u>my</u> letter!) Poor Dorothy! I would like to <u>try</u> & comfort you. Maybe I couldn't cure the "flu" though. I hope you'll be alright again by this time. "flu" is rotten. I'll quite understand if I don't hear for the next days. You should have several of my letters coming to you. [*Dorothy's diary for 25 October, 1918 mentions the death of a young cousin from double pneumonia following 'flu.*]

I agree with you about the boots. They always think people have narrow feet (I think it must be the "thing" to have feet like that). I'm always assured they fit & I get very cross. They hardly ever have a boot the right width for me so I have to get the half size larger in order to get width. So Daft of them. It has always struck me that Belfast boot shops aren't much use.

There's a young rat in my cupboard here. I got a glass down on him once, but he got away and is back again, the cheeky thing. I am sorry I wasn't there to kiss you goodnight & "tuck you in". Do you go in for these Zepp-raid nightsuits? Very fetching – according to the fashion plates! I'm going to have another go at that rat! No good – two of them. I'm getting slow & old you know kid.

Oh I made a little toffee here this evening. For something to do. Quite successful though it was made in a cigarette tin that had been used for putting engine oil on the fire. (First class thing for lighting fires you know engine oil). Shows you what an awful war it is doesn't it? You're not the only one who can cook. I wonder given a Primus or an open fire & army rations which of us could do the best! This isn't intended as an insult! I'm quite convinced you are an excellent cook. That's why I want to marry you of course! I worry such a lot about me "eats". Of course (to be serious) as you say its an advantage but I really want you just because you are your dear self. Nuff said! You know enough – I would like to come along & pet you. Even if you had "flu" or without it!

Goodnight you darling
John S. Riggs

15 November, 1917

Dorothy dear,

I have made many attempts to write this but so far failed. Now I have only time for a note. I have not sent in any papers for the R.F.C. I am just off to the O.P. & have only a second. Will write fully later.

Yours, John S. Riggs

17 November, 1917

Dear Dorothy,

This is a rather late reply to yours of the 6th & 8th, but I have been on 24 hour O.P. & had no chance to write there. And I really don't know what to say now I am writing.

As I told you in my last note. I won't put in any papers for the R.F.C. as long as you think it would be unkind. I didn't think you would object when I thought of it.

Well to answer your first letter. You seem to think that you go on courses to learn things – not at all. That is perhaps what was intended at first, but it really means a rest & getting away from the war for a bit.

Sorry you don't like bullies. I wasn't in any temper we just enjoyed having a scrap at times. You may not know that Ledlie is jolly strong & I am not going to hurt her just to satisfy you. It would be necessary to do so to teach her different. I'm pleased to hear you recovered from 'flu so easily. I don't think its such a lot to be proud of that you recovered quicker than your mother. You aren't so old and you would expect young people to get better sooner.

I'm afraid no effort of mine makes any difference to my leave. I thought I explained you go in turn and no effort makes any difference unless you take someone else's place. They also, strange to say, want leave. And I have only just been three months in the country.

Your second letter. Why I want to rush off with another job? To start with the branch I was going to is not so "disgustingly risky". I am no hero and have not the least desire to die just yet. And I am not settled in this one. I dislike the work & the major here. I know I would have liked the other so naturally I thought of transfer. Yes I remember quite well what I was giving up, and the branch I thought of then wasn't the same as now.

I quite expect you will not understand. And indeed I thought several times if it was worthwhile explaining. You see you regard flight as a most risky thing whereas it isn't. It's only the Hun who makes it the least risky. And I considered that it was equally risky on the ground. Anyhow my luck was my luck & I was content to trust it. I told your mother in a note I wrote some time ago. I haven't heard from her since. Also you would never have seen me in R.F.C. clothes as you still remain with your own corps. I am wondering if everything I do must be considered as to its kindness to you. Another thing. You know that after the war I'll be quite useless & will have to start afresh. Well I thought if I was a qualified pilot it would always be something. Anyway as there will be plenty of work in flight afterwards I think you'll very likely be disappointed in me when I do get leave. You most likely think things about me because I'm away that you wouldn't have the chance to if I was there. Doubt if you'll understand that. Well anyhow my R.F.C. form has not gone. Haddon goes on leave tonight I believe and the Major is to go on a course. I am still forward only they sent another man (the only one of course that no one gets on with very well) to keep me company. The battery moved a little distance away & we were left in charge of our respective guns up here.

We've got the sidecar here & may look for a run now the Major is gone. I've had my machine here of course all the time though it's no use to me. But if I leave it everyone else rides it & usually breaks things. So I keep it by me. I've nothing more to say really, and must write to Nina & your mother.

Yours, John S. Riggs

20 November, 1917

Dearest,

I've just received & read yours of the 12th Nov. Many thanks for it. I meant to write again before I heard but we have been busy. I am just having a quiet battle with the Hun myself now. He (the Hun) has been awfully good about it. Let me win every time. He's such a little gentleman.

I'm really awfully pleased to get your letter. Don't quite know why. About the R.F.C. I have decided to do nothing just now at any rate. I'll wait for my leave and I'll talk to you about it. I have already explained that I'm not in the least anxious to get killed.

And there's nothing wrong with your treatment of me. (Except of course that you are entirely lacking in respect for ME).

Oh I'm dying to have that tie. I've only one at present & its looking rather weak & ill poor thing. I've already explained that there would be no change in my uniform, but I won't use that as an argument. You'll be sorry to hear the Major didn't go on course to England after all. I want this to go out on tonight's post and its nearly time to have a battle again! Well *enfant* dearest, leave isn't much nearer. There's one man in the battery to go before me & he may go any day. He's with me here, but I doubt if anyone can be spared as we have several "on course" (learning? nothing) and he will likely have to wait three weeks or so. And then I come any time after that. Maybe a month, maybe a week

By the way I never had the P.C. Maybe its on the way. So I did worry!

Yes I'm quite sure they are all your letters only I couldn't use ribbon. I use a cycle tube which cuts up nicely into rubber bands. You really [are] a little devil! Yes & I'm sure your mother would agree! I had her letter today too by the way & hope to write to her tonight. You never sent me that stocking! I'm spending money awful fast just now. Maybe you know it costs more to feed two people than 10 or 12 which is our usual mess with the battery. Still we would rather be here on our own. Though I would have liked one of the other men to come instead of the present. Must stop just now. Write soon.

Yours ever, John S. Riggs

21 November, 1917

Dear Mrs Kendall,
   Your very welcome letter received two days ago. I was rather busy one day & the other just lazy. Yes just that.
   About the R.F.C. I gather that Dorothy doesn't like it & I'm going to wait till I get leave to talk to her. That's best. But it puts me, as you can guess, at an awful disadvantage.
   About the Bank. I had an idea you know because mother never even mentioned it to me. I don't think she means anything. Just doesn't understand me or think I can be serious. I'm afraid I always avoid any serious subject with her. And I think she was rather hurt I wouldn't tell her more about it. I don't know why, I just couldn't. And yet you (the girl's mother) were told quite early – or at least knew. (I think you were told weren't you?) I don't understand mother at all. But I feel somehow she is trying to get me to consult her sort of before she would do anything. Well I won't.
   As I say I don't think she means anything, and I can't recall her ever welcoming anyone very heartily. (Just her manner I think). I'm really very sorry to hear you've been laid up. I hope you made that monkey Dorothy look after you. You can't go to German Baths now that's really the thing to do. Or was, wasn't it? But I hope you won't be troubled again. It <u>is</u> rotten to be sick.
   I don't think you are finding fault with my mother. You see she never sort of admitted anything to me, I didn't say anything because it doesn't worry <u>me</u>, but it annoys me rather if she shows anything to either you or Dorothy. I'll have to try & convince her I'm serious when I get leave. Hope you'll write again, I really like your letters you know.
                                                            Yours, John S. Riggs

21 November, 1917

Dorothy dearest,
   This should reach you either the day before, on, or the day after your birthday. So many happy returns. And though you can't go more charming, let's hope you get more respect for ME. Otherwise you know we'll lead an awful life. Do think of it this way. Be terrible if I had to arrive late at work because I'd been slapping you – and that's really what you want at times – or shaking.
   Honestly girl dear. You <u>are</u> a darling. <u>Quite</u> the nicest girl <u>I</u> know. Maybe you'll say that isn't much but I'm awful wise even if I don't know many girls. And quite qualified to judge! (Better not say any more. She'll begin to think things). Ahem!
   I'm glad you can sympathise about the R.F.C. Because when I talk to you, well its not like writing (is it?) and you will most likely get your way. Till then the subject drops. And I don't think somehow I would go if you really object when I've explained. I'm very troubled that the letter before my last will have hurt you. I'm humbly sorry dear if it did. I <u>was</u> rather cross. You seemed to say no without thinking that I <u>had</u> already thought of you. And I do want to be

kind to you *enfant*. Honestly I'll try. So please forgive me this time. It's nearly 11 p.m. I must toddle to bed. I wish I could have sent you something for your birthday, but I haven't been far enough back to get anything decent. And then I'm always afraid that it won't be decent but just rubbish. Anyway think of the value you have in me! I don't love you any less *Enfant*, and you don't know how much I do.

Good night chum, Yours John S. Riggs

22 November, 1917

Dear Girl,

Yours of the 14th just received. I have just time to scribble a note before the post goes. You never answered my question re fashion plates. I forget quite what it was now, but I'm sure there was something important.

No, the toffee thank you was quite good. I ate it all. So that proves it doesn't it. As you remark a hen party is a waste. Now if you would only hold it out here there would be hundreds killed in the rush! Yes, you will certainly be taken whenever anything comes to the Opera. I like going you know – only not to the Gods. I like to see & hear things in a little comfort & you don't get much in the Gods. Anyway you can count that settled. Next please. Oh, do you intend to live in Belfast always? Because I couldn't state yet where I'm going. I think I have enough clothing etc. You see it's not like D.R.ing when you were out most of the time on the roads. Now most of the time I'm indoors and usually have a fire. So I'm quite alright thanks. Well I'm quite capable of looking after myself. You seem to think I'm not. Well marry me and see!

No Haddon isn't like your sketch. He's more like me in build & clean shaven – about 38 I believe. I'll try & raise a photo sometime, but he's on leave at present.

Well I haven't anything more to answer. You'll be 21 when you get this. It is 21 isn't it? When do you expect to get the Vote? Oh I forgot you don't or didn't believe in it do you? I do you know. Shall we have a battle about it?

Your letter came by the way while I was talking to an American doctor down by the guns. He's fed up already! Still he hasn't much to growl about yet. This must go.

Yours, John S. Riggs

28 November, 1917

Dear Girl,

I am sorry I was a beast when I wrote you that letter. I <u>was</u> cross but it didn't last long. And I quite saw that from your point of view you were right. And you aren't a selfish pig. I do feel a brute when you call yourself names that I deserve. You see *enfant* I <u>did</u> think of you before I decided to apply. And I was satisfied with myself that there wasn't anything for you to object to. That was chiefly what made me mad. That you took for granted I never thought of you and needed reminding.

I can quite see you hate it still and are only agreeing to please me. Well that isn't good enough. It might have been at first, but not after saying no. You see when I said I wouldn't send in any papers I meant it. And it meant me killing all interest I had in flying. That was <u>very</u> hard (how hard you don't know) and now when you say "you can if you like" I haven't the same keenness. It's rotten to get that way but I do at times – I lose interest in everything.

I'm trying to explain and you mustn't think anything I raise is to hurt you. Honestly I couldn't be cross with you for long and I recovered long ago. As I have said, and I think its better to stick to this, I wouldn't put in papers till I see you. I don't know if that will do any good but maybe you would like it. I'm not keen on talking about it just now myself, but I must try to explain.

You see I didn't want to confess I disliked this job till I got out of it. I would rather be back D.R.ing again, but that can't be done. And I tried you see for R.F.C. in 1916. Only they wouldn't have me then. There wasn't the demand for recruits you know. I'm afraid I did misunderstand everything you said. There wasn't any excuse for that at all. And I can only be sorry & feel a brute. I'm afraid you made an awful bad choice Dorothy.

It's just the same battery as I joined. And most of the subs and the captain are quite friendly. That is if you can be friends with them. The O.C. [?] always makes a good impression (he believes in that) but nothing else. I wish I hadn't mentioned the work etc. now. Only you wanted reasons & I was cross so I gave one anyway. I'm quite sure you think you understand, I doubt if you do really. I haven't the tone of voice you know to go by. It's very hard trying to write all these things.

Oh *enfant* dear – there's nothing to forgive. And sure your discouraging letters (as you call them) will be forgot. Only I can't change my feelings now. You aren't to blame. Just meself. I can't some way get what I want on paper. I don't quite know myself. Feel as if I'd like to throw up you, R.F.C., R.G.A. and everything. And yet I know I don't want anything more than you. I feel I haven't the necessary courage to take up or do anything you object to. And that's so hopeless because it means we get just nowhere. I've learned that you have always to be giving up & going without in this rotten world. And it makes you quite ready to give everything unless you are prepared to fight for things & risk things. Kipling has it somewhere:

> "If you can make a heap of all your winnings
> And risk it on a throw of pitch & toss – etc"

Well I feel that it's the only way, to chance fate and believe you'll win. Oh this is rot. I won't write more. You are a good kid, but you can't be expected to stand this.

Re notice in papers: I should just post the same if I were you. The chances being that a small mail will cross and as nearly everyone will not write, there will only be a small one. In any case they would only be delayed. I am in two minds to send this or not. It will mean nothing because I can't put it into words. I think I will. You can see the attempt anyway. I believed in your good wishes so much that I couldn't get seriously hurt. And now some way its gone snap. I can't explain. It just isn't there now and I get savage. I'm afraid I'm a bad tempered animal, girl.

You may remember when I came home first that I said I was different. Well I never thought I would return to that when there was you. But that's how I feel about things just now. I'll get over it I guess.

I would like you here just for a bit. Only its imposs. And must be endured. Makes one pessimistic when one thinks of another two or three years & no change. If you could only do something. It's the awful waste of time & "peace-time" war that gets on ones nerves. I'm sure you'll think this a terrible "fed up" letter. It's not really. I'm not fed up. Only I must look for something.

I believe most completely in "Kismet" myself. I live & you live just so long. All on the knees of the Gods. And I don't worry. I can't. I wish you could believe the same, but I can't and don't expect it. Well Dorothy dear, you will know how great a fool I am already, but this proves it. Eh! I don't hope for leave before Xmas now. This other sub is still to go. And as the Major is refus-ing leave places when offered to the latter (on account of pressure of work) I don't know when I might get. Before the end of Jan. 1918 I hope if we aren't in another push somewhere. I'm beginning to think it would have been much fairer to you if I had said nothing. Only I couldn't help it dear. And I'm sure I would do it again. There isn't any news. Just the same old war. And your papers will give enough details about that. Oh I've been thinking of "Tanks" if you object to R.F.C. I haven't made any enquiries yet, so you know early. I applied for them on my commiss papers as well as R.A. you know, only they put me here.

I can't write about other things tonight. I do want to talk to you for a few minutes. Oh I wish I was sure you understood. But you really are an *enfant* & I feel an awful brute for worrying you. I'll try not to offend again so on that. Goodnight dearest.

Yours always, John S. Riggs

28 November, 1917

Dearest Girl,

Yours of the 19th first. I was just going to write when your second one 22nd arrived. So I've two in this letter. I can't help writing in "spasms". It just comes that way. I know sometimes I can't write them. I can't for the life of me think what young lady had budding hopes. And I certainly wasn't trifling with her affections. I do wish you'd tell me who it is. So s'nice to have an unknown admirer you know!

Yes, I quite expected you would renounce me. Just the silly thing you would do! I must get this written before Foorte[?] comes back from O.P. He's there today. You see I hate writing or even reading letters when he's about. He has that effect on me. It's very difficult to explain. It's feeling more than any real thing to go on: but I never feel as if you could trust him. The other men have also noticed it, and yet he's really all right.

No, I don't know *Madame Butterfly*. I don't remember having a chance to see it. Re Zoo. Yes we have a puppy <u>not</u> human. Poor old puppy got partly "gassed" the other night and was a very sick puppy for a day or so. Quite all right now thank you!

The family all told me you were at the theatre that night & wouldn't look at them! Yes, I had forgotten about Nina's birthday till too late. As it happens I sent her some money to get me *Punch* & she took some of it for her birthday.

I don't think its possible to train these rats. They are too independent and <u>take</u> what they want. Cuss! Cuss! Cuss! Have just been visited by the Colonel and we'll have to shift our quarters from the château I'm afraid. We're about 300 yards forward of the guns & it won't do. Awful. Just when we were fixed up! Re Face Fungus – you know of course that No. 2 is the most popular! I go in for a modified form! Still its only temporary. I'll likely have it off on the first sign of Blighty! Your second letter – I've been interrupted several times since writing the above. And I'm getting so cross – I hate to be disturbed when I'm writing to anyone. I'll have to let this go now. It's so late it will only just catch the post. Foorte came back from O.P. but has now gone for the evening to a concert at the Squadron. I'll see him tomorrow again. So I'll have the evening clear to write you enfant. Cheerio till later.

John S. Riggs

30 November, 1917

Dorothy dear,

I wrote you an awful lot of nonsense last night. I don't want you to pay any attention to it. Because I'm quite all right this morning. I wish now I hadn't sent it. But I get moods at times and everything's rather rotten for a while. So you suffered. I'll try not to let it happen again. I don't know what to do about the R.F.C. I know you don't want me to & yet I think that if I don't put in papers you'll think I'm trying to rub it in. I'm not. But if you are going to worry all the time I don't see how I'm to do it. I wish I could convince you that there isn't anything more to worry about.

And I wouldn't hate you if I don't go. Don't be silly – I wish it didn't take so long to get answers to ones letters. I can't expect to hear till about Xmas now if this ten days stoppage comes off. Then it will be anything up to two months before a transfer gets through. I feel inclined to chance it. Because maybe they won't accept it. And that would settle it. And you may really agree. In which case it might as well be put in now. I feel you know that you will say yes & really mean no. And that's worse than nothing.

I can't write decently just now because this other man is wandering about & asking daft questions. Whether I want matches etc. from A— or something equally silly. I expect I'll be on O.P. tomorrow so I shan't have any chance then.

Time seems to go slower here than any of the other places. B.C. posts & going up & down to O.P.S. Nothing new ever happens. Or if it does I's only for a little while & then the same old round. I think I'll run into A— for a change. See some friends, have lunch & come back. Awful war! Well I don't know what to do. Maybe your next letter will decide. If I could only be sure you wouldn't worry I'd go like a shot. You know if you wanted to do anything like that I wouldn't mind. I could believe that it was all right because I know the chances are always against anything happening. Oh I'm sick of this subject.

Really nothing to write about. Seems ages since I heard. Isn't really you know. Three days I think. I'm quite incapable of writing. Maybe when I get back – but that won't be this post.

John S. Riggs

7 December, 1917

Dear Girl,

Yours of the 26/11 first. I've been busy the last two or three days and couldn't get settled down to write to you. It's possibly because our mails from this section now go by a field battery near us that they take longer. You see we haven't any means of stamping or sending them off so the neighbouring battery does it. And they may let our mails lie for a day or so before they send them on.

You'll be pleased to hear that Foorte has gone on his leave, and I've had the captain down here till Haddon came back. Haddon just arrived here today. Yes, his family all well thank you! I am next for leave in the battery anyway & I believe only two or three down the group list. You see the leave comes from the Group list. I hope with luck to be home in January.

Re evening dress in the last portion of your letter. I quite agree with you. I think it's fierce – and tall hats! Had quite a decent evening with Haddon. We always get something to talk about & as we differ on several subjects can always raise an argument. And we had one game of chess! It was a very serious game. I'm afraid I get awful fed up with this old war at times & want to come back and marry you. Strange sort of wish isn't it? I wonder can you see me now. Writing at a table for once & holding an argument with Haddon now & then. Unlaced field boots, no collar or tie and unbuttoned tunic because I've got so fat. Awful. I'm sure you'll give me up. This isn't in answer to your last letter. I'll write that later, and one to your mother whose letter came today.

Well, for tonight girl – I am looking for this leave. I hope it will be soon.

Yours always, John S. Riggs

8 December, 1917

Dorothy dearest,

Yours of the 28th to answer. Many thanks for enclosing your grandfather's letter. He does seem a decent old gent. But how he can tell such a lot about me with nothing to go on I don't know.

You don't really think I'm inquisitive do you? It's just my thirst for knowledge you know! I thought & hoped you would come along with me (if she doesn't know she's wanted by this time! – well she never will.)

I'm certain your birthday blouse must have been nice. I'm quite looking forward to seeing all these swagger turnouts. They'll be quite fresh to me no matter how old you think them. I don't understand my family myself. Because though they said Bob McIntyre was somewhere round Arras they didn't say where, and I've had to ask. Of course you must remember that they don't understand maps, so your showing Nina wouldn't, I'm afraid, convey anything. I know I wasn't awfully good about the R.F.C. I was a bad tempered brute.

I wonder could I send you anything for Xmas. The only thing is money. Maybe you could buy something you want & let me. There is a very faint chance of my getting home for Xmas. I told you in yesterday's letter that I was likely to go any time now. That would settle it. But if I'm not would you let me?

Hurrah – a wisdom tooth! Sure you won't be able to contain yourself with sinful pride! Rotten about your knee – I'll have to think out a treatment for it. Then you'll refuse to have it treated. I expect this isn't much of a letter in return for yours but really I seem to have nothing to say. Thoughts of leave unsettle me. I'm off into A— for an hour or two. I'm on O.P. tomorrow.

Yours always, John S. Riggs

11 December, 1917

Dear Mrs Kendall,

I received your last letter today in your parcel. Many thanks. I didn't quite know what to do with myself (like a dog with two tails) when I have a letter from Dorothy, one from you & a parcel. You're jolly decent to me and I feel I don't deserve it.

Yes, I realise quite what was packed into the box, and I'm very grateful. The books are most welcome, as we have a lot of time on our hands when you may be called on and don't want to start anything serious. I'll certainly tell you what I think of them. Well one, *The Forest Lovers*, I've read and liked muchly, but it was so long ago that I'm looking forward to reading it again.

I hadn't noticed that Dorothy felt any more cos of the R.F.C. She conceals her feelings very well. Too well sometimes. Because I'm an unbelieving animal I really think you hold mistaken ideas of the F.C. They don't fly every day or even every week. I forgot for a second when I mentioned the puppy getting gassed that you weren't used to it. Bless you there's nothing in gas. Not nowadays. Just uncomfortable while it's on. No more unless, which very seldom happens, it takes you unawares.

Your good wishes for Xmas certainly are in time. Nevertheless you know I welcome them. I'll delay mine for a while. There is a faint chance of leave at Xmas. Rather faint. I don't count on anything now but shall be very glad if anything comes off.

Re Dorothy & the R.F.C. again. I'm not going to hurt her feelings for sure, but I think that it would take something to hurt her. Seems always a kid to me and a kid just howls & forgets.

Now your letter that came before the parcel one – Nov. 29ᵗʰ. I've already said I think you have a mistaken idea of the R.F.C. Still I can explain that on the much expected leave. I think A.S.C., A.A.T. people do get fed up easily. They don't get the touch to keep interest alive in this old war. I know our M.T. people are always fed up. Never can decide if they'll go to Amiens or St. Pol today! No honestly, I'm sorry to hear your brother's disappointed again. He had several over his last leave didn't he?

This knee of Dorothy's doesn't look well. May take a long time. Rather rotten. And I'm sure you blame me for letting her ride that bike. But what defence had I?

I am pleased to hear you enjoyed your stay in bed. Sure its <u>my</u> only pleasure left in the army. They lop off everything one by one, but bed! Yes, I'm sure Dorothy does look well in bed. I don't think though she would like your remark except from her sinful pride which shouldn't be encouraged. I have my work cut out as it is. Sorry I can't make any remark on the Cambrai push. Just as well maybe. I am in hopes of leave before the end of January. Not so far away though it seems so. It's 11 pip emma so I must to bed.

John S. Riggs

11 December, 1917

Dorothy dearest,

I don't quite know where to start. When I came up from the guns this morning for lunch there were two letters <u>and</u> a parcel & the parcel contained another from your mother. I have just read the lot & am now writing with my feet on the stove (to aid thought!). Really jolly decent of you to write three – and as Haddon remarked (with truth) when he saw the way my parcel was put together said "You aren't worth it". I was afraid to open some of the things for fear of "spoiling" your ribbons. I can't hope to answer all your letters in one dear girl, but I'll send this as proof of intent to answer them later.

First very many thanks for the parcel – really splendid of you. I'm very pleased & grateful – you are a good *enfant*. Yes I know "Eve" – very popular here you know. Poor *enfant*. Only "Navy Cut" to smoke. Well you know you shouldn't so it brings its own punishment. [*Dorothy was asthmatic and later in life detested smoke and smokers!*]

I'm sorry about my mother to you. You see we haven't been exactly in touch with one another & I couldn't tell her about you beforehand. So I think she was hurt or disappointed I didn't tell her or something. I'll try & make her realise I am serious when I get leave. I think she might be more "friendly" but she hasn't been even to me for ages. It's very hard to explain. She believes such funny things of me. Do you know she asked me seriously once how many times I'd killed people on the roads! I'm glad you don't worry because I can't do anything. I'm too proud of you to attempt to prove anything about you to anyone even my mother. If she doesn't understand it's almost impossible to make her.

Many, many thanks for the tie *enfant*. Makes me feel ashamed when you're so good. And it's a great tie – I'll keep it for leave I think – too swagger for here. Yes, the date box is fine. Really my cheild you – dear! Well I must let this go. I'll write tonight.

Cheerio Dorothy darling, John S. Riggs

11 December, 1917

Dear Girl,

Yours of the 4th is the next one. I don't know why my letters should take so long, but I expect this Field Battery who takes ours has a lot to do with it. You see they wouldn't worry if ours missed a few posts.

I confess. I did think that you wouldn't mind where I went and I couldn't see why you should. It's not that I don't believe you when you say you care. It's not Dorothy. But I can't realise that you are interested where I go. Because you see it's all the army to me and I hate it. It's just something that has to be done and I want to get as much adventure out of it as I can. There are so many things I want to do & this is is just wasting time.

It is talking rot when I grouse. It's not the game, and doesn't alter things a bit. And being serious is worse I think – one's got to keep on laughing. I can't always though. Chiefly because of "got to". I hate things you <u>must</u> do as a rule. And I can't really trouble you with my grouses you know – you <u>are</u> an *enfant* and it's not right. I can't get it into words quite. There isn't really anything else to answer in your letter. You're an awfully good girl to take so much trouble. And I'm very very grateful. You can't know what it means to me. It's so much I find it hard to believe. You mustn't be cross if I sometimes can't believe. Because most times I do – just now and then reason asserts itself and I'm sure I'm a pig to you. Oh, that calendar you sent – you did it yourself didn't you?

There doesn't seem anything else to say in answer to that letter. Leastways there is a lot to <u>say</u> only I can't write it. Sort of at the back of my mind. Yes, I <u>have</u> a mind of sorts. Best I can do I'm afraid. I wish I could really tell you some of my thoughts. Only I'm afraid. You aren't serious often you know and you seldom, very very seldom, let me see when you are. I can't help but keep thoughts to myself at times, because I feel you won't listen. You will I <u>know</u> when I think about it. It's just I'm more used to keeping silent about the things that really move me. Do you see? I think you will somehow.

Your second letter of the 4th. You do write jolly fine letters girl dear, and very welcome ones. I can only be sorry if you get absent minded, must be awful! Your sketch of the unknown seems familiar somehow – I must have seen the original somewhere. I <u>have</u> a lot to thank you for. You can't claim you did it on purpose, but still I thank you.

Oh the pup got quite well again thank you. Sure we forgot it hadn't a gas bag. Gas doesn't worry me really you know – only uncomfortable, but much better now than it used to be. It's only dangerous when it gets you unawares.

The shift to our other quarters hasn't come off yet; will shortly though, and we won't be sorry. We'll be below ground there & its much warmer in winter. This place is full of holes. It's a gentleman (leastways we'll call him that) higher up who is the cause of our shifting. You are correct about the fungus. Only I said a modified pattern so there is no call for "low" (yes "low" Miss Kendall) remarks. Sure it's only temporary & I cut bits every day to keep it in its place. Do give the thing a chance. You won't have to bear it!

No, I'm not going to cremate your letters – not unless you want me to. I don't see why you should? I can manage all right. Well I must rise me at 6 ack emma the morn's morn and I want to write to your mother. I'm afraid her letter will be short.

You'll thank Rosemary for the crackers for me – I'll send her a card later. Rather chilly this weather we have an inch of ice and a leetle snow. Enough to remind us of winter. P.B.I. [*Poor Bloody Infantry*] we are all right. They are really heroes. Well it's a long way off Xmas yet. Fortnight. And that other sub is due back about the 20th. So if by any lucky chance the next date was just after he got back I might manage Xmas. Sheer luck though. You see I don't expect the O.C. to let me go till he comes back. Not that I couldn't but just that's the way of it.

Oh I've borrowed a Decca here & about 20 records so we'll be noisy. One doesn't call it music quite but it's a noise and passes time. Haddon & I have one game of chess in an evening usually so you see how groundless your fears were! Well I really must go. Good night girl dearest.

You're all the world to me Dorothy,
Yours John S. Riggs

This poem copied in Dorothy's handwriting was among the obitiuaries and letters of condolence.

Knowledge
by Peggy Fraser

I never knew until you won my heart
How a great love could alter and make fair,
How joy could radiate from face and form,
And leave the promise of more beauty there.
I never knew until you touched my hair
How strong a thrill could flood through heart and mind,
How just the tenderness of Love's caress
Could reach my soul and round my life-springs wind
I never knew that Life was rich and full
Until one day you drew me to your heart
And held me there and pressed your lips on mine,
Vowing that I was yours, till Death should part
But now I know that Life may wear a crown;
That heaven-born joys may thrill a human frame;
That neither Death itself nor things of earth
Can ever dim the glow of Love's bright flame.